Tabu Creations

Book of Poetry

*(poems that will uplift you, expand your mind,
give you comfort and much more)*

Mr. & Mrs. Grier,
    I thank God for allowing our paths to
cross and also giving me the opportunity
to be able share my gift with you. I pray
that my poems uplift and inspire you.
                                    Love
                                    Tabu

Author: Tomeeka "Tabu" Beaver

Xulon PRESS

Tabu Creations
Book of Poetry
by Tomeeka "Tabu" Beaver

Printed in the United States of America

ISBN 9781622308620

www.xulonpress.com

I dedicate this book to my children
Javon and Tamia
You can do anything that you put your mind to

Acknowledgments

*F*irst I would like to thank my heavenly Father for blessing me with the gift of writing, for giving me the words and wisdom to help expand minds, touch hearts and help spiritual growth. I thank my husband, Alonzo, for his support and love. I thank those family members, friends and pastors that gave me the much needed support and foundation to step out in faith and share my gift with you. I would also like to thank my lovely MOVA Sistas. Put this on our book list ladies. My prayer has always been to touch millions across the world with my poetry and I'm claiming it done. . .so let's begin.

Much love and many blessings to you,

Tabu

Psalms 45:1- My heart overfloweth with a goodly matter; I speak the things which I have made touching the king: My tongue is the pen of a ready writer.

THE ANOINTING HAS A HOLD ON ME

I am a changed woman
I now walk in His name
And my steps do not falter
The path is endless
And I continue
For Him
By Him
Through Him
The anointing has a hold on me

My brightness may blind you
Because I glow with His love
And my shine will not dim
Attractive is my light
I bring souls
Touch hearts
Open minds
For Him
The anointing has a hold on me

My words now open your eyes
Because I speak for Him
And continuously they come
Obediently I write
I share
I give
I read
The message from Him
To you
The anointing has a hold on me

Table of Contents

xv

Chapter 1

"Anointed"

PHILIPPIANS 4:13

My life. . .
I used to direct it my way
Ignored what the Word would say
I got this
But I kept falling
Failing
Got tired of wailing
Had to rethink my direction
I was on my way to destruction
Nothing was right
All was wrong
I was becoming weak
But I started strong
I think
Maybe that was a delusion
Intrusion
On my thoughts
The devil had me
I was caught
But someone was praying
Wow! For me
But things got worse
As the devil tried to keep his grip on me
But I remembered
As a child what I heard
The pastor saying
All I need is in the Word
I searched
I looked
For that special book
You know, the Bible
Which I neglected for years
Once found
Its condition brought me to tears
Out fell a page
And all I could see
I can do all things through Christ
Who strengthens me
Philippians 4:13

Now hangs on my wall
I now put God first
And He never allows me to fall
My wrongs are made right
My Bible never leaves my sight
I'm on my way to life ever more
This I am sure
My life. . .

JESUS IS IN ME

I smile
because the devil is funny.
He tries to affect
my heart, my family, my money,
not realizing
that Jesus is in me!

I stand on the word
which gives me power,
every second;
every hour.
Jesus is in me!

He places my enemies
beneath my feet.
He gives me strength
for those who try to make me weak.
Yes,
Jesus is in me!

He gives me favor
in times of drought.
Confused are those
who don't know what He's about.
Yes,
Jesus is in me!

So I laugh
because the devil sure is funny,
he doesn't realize that I've swallowed the Word
which is sweater than honey.

THE DEVIL DOESN'T UNDERSTAND

He must not know where I'm standing.
On the Word!
He must not see that things have changed.
I am a new creation!
He must not know where I reside.
I live but I am not of this world!
He must think I can still be persuaded.
I have too much knowledge!
He has no clue that I am no longer lost.
I have been found!
He must think that I am still weak.
I have renewed strength!
He still thinks I can be tempted by money.
I know prosperity is mine!
He can't know who lives on the inside.
Jesus!

YOU HAVE A CHOICE

Have you heard about the man who gave His life for us?
He took the ridicule, the beatings and the spitting without a complaint or fuss.
He was innocent; He didn't do a single thing.
He died for our sins; the lies, the murder, fornication and slandering.
There was more but the list is much too long.
How can someone turn their back on the one who died for their wrongs?
I'm confused! That was love in its most purest form.
A life was given so that you can be reborn,
And have another chance to live this life right.
You should be on your knees thanking Him every day and night.
Tell Him that you love Him, open your mouth and give Him some praise.
Show Him in your worship; lift your head and let your hands be raised,
To the one that our Father laid down for us.
He is awesome! He is almighty! His name is Jesus.
If you're a witness and you love Him, let me hear you lift your voice,
If you don't know Him now you know, take Him in your heart you have a choice.

LISTEN TO THIS TESTIMONY

Listen to this testimony that I'm bringing to you
I thought my life was over, I thought I was through
The devil was attacking me my body as a whole
He was tugging and pulling trying to take my soul
As I read the Word he took away my vision
As I searched for alternatives he confused my decisions
So I started buying cd's to end his game
Little did he know I was still calling on the name
Jesus, the healer who would make this right
The more I called His name the less I had to fight
Now I stand before you with the ability to see
Cause I never gave up and kept Jesus close to me
Jesus is a healer and that's a fact
You can't defeat me devil so get off my back
I'm Holy Ghost filled you can't string me along
I'm built on the Word and my foundation is strong

Listen to this testimony that I'm bringing to you
I thought my life was over, I thought I was through
The devil was attacking me my job and my money
Told me to stop tithing, now ain't that funny
I was no longer working and I lost my home
Tried calling on my friends but no one picked up the phone
But little did he know I'm not a quitter I'm a giver
Reading Malachi 3 I knew who would deliver
Jesus, the provider who gives it all
The more I called His name He wouldn't allow me to fall
Now I stand before you with a house that's much bigger
Cause I never gave up, Jesus blessed my dollar figures
Jesus is a provider and that's a fact
You can't defeat me devil so get off my back
I'm Holy Ghost filled you can't string me along
I'm built on the Word and my foundation is strong

Listen to this testimony that I'm bringing to you
I thought my life was over, I thought I was through
The devil was attacking me, my spouse and my kids
Had me second guessing all the things that I did
Did I make the right choices, were they holding me back

He started filling my head with a whole 'lotta' smack
I started leaning on the Word and not my own understanding
Started reaching for the one whose love is undemanding
Jesus, the best thing that's ever happened to me
The more I called His name the more He reconstructed me
Now I stand before you with a heart that's much stronger
Cause I never gave up Jesus made my love longer
Jesus is a lover and that's a fact
You can't defeat me devil so get off my back
I'm Holy Ghost filled you can't string me along
I'm built on the Word and my foundation is strong

HE'LL DO FOR YOU

He'll talk to you when your friends are too busy
He'll talk to you when your spouse doesn't notice you
He'll talk to you when your phone calls are unanswered

He'll protect you when the enemy strikes
He'll protect you when you've lost your direction
He'll protect you in all situations

He'll comfort you when the tears won't stop
He'll comfort you through pain and suffering
He'll comfort you when you feel alone and no one cares

Jesus will do these things because He cares for you
Jesus will do these things because He loves you
Jesus will do these things because He wants you to have life everlasting

GOODBYE DRUGS

I have no need for you anymore
I am speaking over my body
There is no longer a need for
Covering insecurities
Hurt and pain
I have accepted Jesus in my life
And no longer bow my head in shame
I no longer depend on a chemical high
I'm now enjoying a spiritual high
So drugs
In my life you no longer serve a purpose
Goodbye

THINKING ABOUT YOU

Lord I was sitting here thinking today
And I realized all that I've asked for
You've given me
Not the next day
And for some
Not the next week or year
But right on time
When you felt I needed them
And I thank you
You are an awesome and loving God
Sometimes we can get so busy with life
That we don't even see the blessings received
Or take the time to recognize you
For giving them
So once again
I come before you
To honor and praise your name
And to say thank you
I love you

SOUND MIND

Sickness you can't have me
I rebuke you in the name of Jesus
I'm claiming healing
So you won't see me complain or fuss
I know my lord
Is true to his word
To allow the devil to defeat me
Would be absurd
So back off me
You can't pull me down
My heart is in Jesus
So my mind is sound

STRUGGLE

I struggle daily Father
To hold on to you
To feel you
To walk like you
But my flesh is weak
So I ask you for strength
And thank you for your patience
I really don't enjoy this struggle
It seems like when I take a positive
Step forward
The devil pulls me back two
And sometimes I allow it
For this I am ashamed
Because I already knew
That without you I'm vulnerable to sin
So I'm coming back to you
Asking for forgiveness
Asking to be reborn in you
I'm putting my past behind me
So I can live for you

SMILE FOR YOU

Some will smile because of a position they hold
What they don't understand is my smile is true. . .bold
In you Lord for what you do
And have done for me
I smile for all to see
The joy in my praise
The strength in the hands I raise
The confidence in my walk
The truth in my talk
My faith in your word
Regardless of what the world may have heard
All that I am and have is because of you
I will continue to show and present my love to you

WINNERS IN HIM

You're not going to get far
Without Jesus near to your heart
You'll think you're getting somewhere
Then find yourself right back at the start
Of your problems, your hurt,
Your pain
Without Jesus
There is no gain
Just accept Him into your life
Repent from your sins
Do it in faith and honesty
And watch your new life begin
Speak over your sickness
You will be healed
Ask for protection
And your enemies will be revealed
Joy will replace sadness
I'm telling you
He'll get rid of all your madness
But you have to be willing
You have to make the first move
In Jesus we are all winners
And with Satan you're sure to lose

HE DID IT FOR US

Close your eyes
You see murder and lies
You see envy and hate
You see a world that can't even have a decent debate
You see a world where it's common for a man to look at a man
You know, the same way that I look at my man
You're seeing women going from one man's bed to another
You see children no longer obeying their fathers and mothers
And honoring our leaders, you no longer see
To say sex sells is an understatement, just turn on your TV

Now open your eyes and picture your child
He or she is being sacrificed for every sin that has been filed. . .before God
Those things you pictured in your mind
Those things that made you cringe at times
Things your child never did
Is your LOVE great enough to give your child for these people to live

I know of one. . .
AWESOME is our Father
He did that for us. . .
"Jesus"

Give GLORY to our Father, He did that for us. . .
"Jesus"
Give HONOR to our Father, He did that for us. . .
"Jesus"
Give PRAISE always to our Father, because he did that for us
"And his name is Jesus"

I LOVE THE NEW ME

I used to walk through life
With no direction or purpose
The paths were many
It was hard to focus
Left or right
I was lost
Paying the cost
For trying to do it my way
Nah, you can't bring me back to those days
"I love the new me"

I used to run the streets
Feeding my body worldly fun
Did everything under the sun
Plenty to get in
Plenty of sin
Didn't know
I was starvin' my soul
Nah, I don't miss those days of not feeling whole
"I love the new me"

I used to chase the dollar
Lookin' for ways to get rich
Pay bills. . .provide meals
Ya know, my sales pitch
My hustle
But I was broke
Runnin' numbers was a joke
Didn't know prosperity was mine
Nah, I'm not going back to chasin' a dime
"I love the new me"

I used to go around lookin' for friends
Who wouldn't let me be a part
Of their group, their click
It broke my heart
I was lonely
Often wanted to die
There was no one to talk to, didn't fit in. . .why

Had no clue Jesus was callin' me to come hang with Him
Nah, you can't pull me away from my best friend
"I love the new me"
That He has created

GOD'S LOVE PURIFIES ME

I'm a child of God
And I represent Him
A soldier, a witness
True bible Christian
The world is scared
Of people like me
I rebuke their songs
Cut off my TV
Keep my mind free
Of sin and destruction
Let God fill my mind
I'm under His construction
He's the builder of my soul
When I fall apart
He takes away my faults
Gives me a new start
My mind is set
On the word that He gave
It gives me direction
Shows me how to behave
Steer away from sin
Always love my neighbor
Honor my parents
Show love to the savior
Kill no one
And rebuke all lust
Save myself for my spouse
And prayer is a must
The word is in my heart
My foundation is strong
With God by my side
I can't go wrong

God's love purifies me
God's love sets me free
There's no greater love for me
God's love, God's love
Purifies me

Don't have to act phony
To keep fake friends
I now chill with those
Who are born again
I'm now rocking to the beat
Of Christian rap and R&B
Moving and dancing
I give all praises to thee
Telling all that I see
On the street and in school
That the devil is a liar
And Jesus is cool
Being a Christian is fun
But I'm really not playing
His love is available
There's no delaying

God's love purifies me
God's love sets me free
There's no greater love for me
God's love, God's love
Purifies me

It purifies me
It can purify you
The decision is yours
So watcha gonna do
The world or Jesus
You can only choose one
Everlasting joy
Or damaging fun
I stand before you
A living testimony
That His love is real
It's extraordinary
So open up your mouth
And sing with us
If you're down with the Father
And the son Jesus

God's love purifies me
God's love sets me free
There's no greater love for me
God's love, God's love
Purifies me

LOVE PURIFIED

Love
One of the strongest feelings that one can show
Love can comfort, love can heal
Love can help one grow
Love touches, love hears
Love speaks
But love can also hurt if your mind is weak
Yea, that's deep
But think, God says keep my word in your mind
But your love for the world takes all your time
Love their music. . .bad thoughts
Love sex. . .diseases are caught
Love their drugs. . .body falls apart
Love their direction. . .you're lost from the start
Love, pure love
Purifies your thoughts, purifies your soul
The world will reach. . .pull
But won't be able to get a hold
Because true love
That is of God, is within you
How strong or weak it is depends on you
Read the word. . .love knowledge grows
Help others. . .love caring shows
Pray constantly. . .love spirit shines
Accept His son. . .love body, soul and mind
Love
Genuine love does not hide
Loving self, loving all, loving God
Is love purified

YOU I ADORE

I used to step out
With no sense of direction
A lost soul
Not under God's protection
I walked through life
Without a purpose or meaning
My joy was careening
I wore myself out; I was part of the world
And I gave it my all
It was fun at first
Then I began to fall
Apart
On my way to my end
But someone shared the word
And my new life began
I had a new purpose
With God by my side
I gave up control
And let Him be my guide
My soul was found
And I have a new walk
My life is better y'all
This is truth, definitely real talk

I walk with you Lord
You I adore
I walk with you Lord
You I adore

I lived the fast life
Always looking for a high
Be it through friends or drugs
I couldn't tell you why
My mind was messed up
I was totally confused
The love that I was giving
Was only being used
I listened to music
That damaged my mind

I drank alcohol
To erase all the grime
The dirt
The evil things that I did
The thoughts were plenty
That ran through my head
I was reaching for wrong
But I started reaching right
Started calling on the Lord
Kept Him in my sight
He became my joy
He became my high
My world is much better
This I can't deny

I reach for you Lord
You I adore
I reach for you Lord
You I adore

Sad, depressed
That's all that I could feel
Had a few acquaintances
But the friendship wasn't real
There was no one to talk to
When life became rough
Nor a shoulder to lean on
Now tell me that ain't tough
I was by myself
I was dealt the wrong hand
What did I do to be alone
I didn't understand
But I began to pray
And fell to my knees
Asked the Lord to come in
Put my life at ease
He assured me
That He was always by my side
With Him
I can always confide
Now my smile replaces sadness
Cause I have a true friend
To lean on

To talk to
And His love never ends

I smile for you Lord
You I adore
I smile for you Lord
You I adore

I walk with you Lord
(I'm walking with you)
I reach for you Lord
(I reach out my hands)
I smile for you Lord
(Yes, I smile, smile, smile)
You I adore

PRACTICE

Practice and perfect your position in the Lord

Remember to pray that we stay on one accord

Actions are required, not a lazy soul

Christ's name being lifted and shared is our goal

Talk, because communication helps bring success

Ignite your spirit with the Word to help bring out your best

Changing souls for the better is what we plan to do

Everyone's involvement will help us see this through

PROTECT ME, PROTECT YOU

Daddy, you tried to protect me,
From that big world that I wanted to see,
And I apologize for talking back; being grown,
Thought I was missing something, had to see for my own.
So I left the comfort of your house; your arms,
To my so called friends who wowed me with their charm.
I put God to the side; I was ready to have fun,
I was tired of church and hearing about the almighty one.
Prayer and worship was replaced with drugs and drinking,
Knowledge of the Word was no more; sex was all I was thinking,
Shouting a joyful noise became shouts of rage,
I was filled with so much anger and confusion, I no longer looked my age.
I began to wonder, "Who was I? Who did I become?"
Joy was gone, beauty was missing; I looked like a bum.
I was now in and of the world, so full of sin,
I bent my head in shame, fell to my knees and asked God to come back in,
And he said, "Wipe your tears and cry no more,
I never left; just waited for you to reopen your door.
I couldn't force you; you had to do it on your own, so I waited patiently,
Worldly joy is temporary so I knew you'd come running back to me,
And you did, so lift your head and stand up proud.
Your sins are forgiven, the devil can't have you; he's not allowed.
You have accepted me, so now you're mine,
I hear your heart and it yells love pure genuine.
Go out to the world, change souls, share your testimony.
I want you to bring my children, lost and confused, back to me."
So I search, I write and I share,
Do what I was told to do,
So listen! You know who you are.
This message was read today with a purpose to protect you.
Love,
Lost and found child of God.

REACHING

One hand reaches to my past
grasping
remembering the good times
the fun times
how much joy I felt then.

One hand reaches toward my future
stretching
to promises of new feelings
new memories
better times
new growth.

But I struggle within myself
how to pull them together
embrace the two
without hindering my growth.

Confused?
A little
but I know I shouldn't be
because I serve a God who's not about confusion
So I'm leaning on you Lord
In faith
for understanding
for knowledge
to become the child that you want me to be

I'm reaching
for you
and I thank you.

I THANK YOU LORD

I thank you Lord
For reaching in and giving me a new heart

I thank you Lord
For erasing my past and giving me a new start

I thank you Lord
For the new direction as I walk my walk

I thank you Lord
For the new language I speak as I've changed my talk

I thank you Lord
For opening my mind allowing new wisdom to flow through

I thank you Lord
For loving me and I appreciate all that you do

DREAM

I close my eyes and I see
What I wanna be
What I ought to be
What I'm gonna be
Because I dream
And I believe
With hard work
There's nothing I can't achieve
I was born to lead
Have dominion over it all
Yes, struggles will come
But I know who to call
My heavenly Father
Who provides me with wisdom
Provides me with strength
He cheers me on
So I can go the full length
Of my dream
Of my vision
Through His word
I base all my decisions
As I lead
Following the people to His will
Telling the devil to back off
Causing him to be still
And flee
He don't want to mess with me
A spirit filled leader
With a dream
With God
As the captain of my team
I am destined
To prosper and win
Anything
That I put my hand in

VIRTUOUS WOMAN

I am strong
I am confident
And I live my life with purpose
I am a virtuous woman

I speak truth
I share wisdom
And I give love unconditionally
I am a virtuous woman

I pray in faith
Study the word
And I am guided by the Father, Son and Holy Spirit
I am a virtuous woman

My steps follow Jesus
With my voice I shout praise
And I glorify Him with no shame

Yes
This is me
A Virtuous Woman

TRUE VALENTINE

Lord, before your love
I was sin divine,
Couldn't tell me nothing
I felt I was doing fine.
I struggled daily
My life was in a constant grind,
Didn't realize I was lost
Walking a very thin line.

Lord, when I met your love
It blew my mind,
My sins were in battle with righteousness
I was in a bind.
Should I walk down this new path
Leave my joy of doing wrong behind?
I wondered if your love was as pure as I heard;
Was it really genuine?

Lord, as I grew in your love
My spirit inclined.
I was moving in the right direction;
Finally in my prime.
My troubles slowly faded away
No longer was there a reason to whine.
Searching for worldly desires stopped
My spirit was all I wanted to find.

Lord, now that I've accepted and held on to your love
My whole person shines.
I let the world know
That I am yours and you are mine.
I look to you for guidance, study your word
And talk to you all the time.
This love that I feel for you
Is like no other kind.

In my heart I hold you forever
As my one and only true Valentine.

THAT AIN'T NOTHIN' BUT GOD'S LOVE

You feel like you're alone,
The tears constantly fall,
You want to give up,
You've given it your all.
Then all of a sudden
Your spirit is uplifted and the tears all dry.
Joy automatically takes over,
You feel better and don't have to ask why.
"That ain't nothin' but God's love!"

You're in school,
You haven't retained any information.
You study constantly,
You're not able to maintain your concentration.
During test time you're nervous,
But once you lift your pencil answers come in a breeze.
You finish with no problem,
There's no question why your mind was at ease.
"That ain't nothin' but God's love!"

You battle with peer pressure.
Should you do what's wrong or what's right?
You know if you make the wrong decision,
Your friends won't want you in their sight.
You worry, but soon you don't care.
It doesn't matter; with them you're no longer concerned.
A peace comes over you because it's not their judgment that you yearn.
"That ain't nothin' but God's love!"

When you feel alone or want to give up
PRAY!
If you're struggling with school or life
PRAY!
Throughout all your troubles
PRAY!
Talk to your Father, believe,
And He'll fix it in His own way,
"Because that ain't nothin' but God's love!"

I AM A LABORER OF GOD

I am a BUILDER of my foundation,
Blocking out all forms of temptation.
I am a PROOFREADER of my thoughts and words
So no fault can be found in anything you heard.
I am a TEACHER sharing my knowledge with others,
Giving revelation to my sisters and brothers.
I am a laborer of God

I'm a HEALER
Healing with prayer in Jesus' almighty name;
Anytime, anywhere I have no shame.
I'm a RACER
Racing for souls until I hit the finish line,
Because His return is coming;
No one knows the time.
I'm a CLEANER
Cleansing my spirit with daily prayer,
Because sin is rampant and can become a snare.
I am a laborer of God

I work CONSTRUCTION
Building paths that direct to His will,
Warning all to take cautious steps
And know when to be still.
I am a MANAGER
Managing my heart to produce an abundance of love,
To mirror our heavenly Father above.
I am a BODY BUILDER
Strengthening my will by shouting His praise,
On my knees I submit,
My hands I raise.
I am a laborer of God

My number one priority
Is to be promoted by Him

GENERATION X-PLOSION

I'm not down with your crew
What you do
I follow through
With God's word
So forget what ya heard
I know who I am
A mighty bible Christian
Generation X-plosion

Who am I
I am a child of El Shaddai
I am a part of a new day
Living my life the bible way
We sing, we praise
We step, we raise
Our hands
To only one
The Son
True and faithful Christians
Generation X-plosion

We are a generation of believers
And achievers
Tithes we give
His word we live
Everyday
Our generation
We will explode
Take over what you heard
Removing sin
With God we can win
As Generation X-plosion

I PRAYED AND PRAYED

I prayed and prayed this day would come
I even cried, now I shed joyful tears

I prayed and prayed this day would come
And now you'll soon be here

I prayed and prayed this day would come
I can't wait to hold you near

I prayed and prayed this day would come
I will love you, guide you and protect you from fear

I prayed and prayed this day would come
God has us in His favor, this is so very clear

I prayed and prayed this day would come
Our baby a blessing that we'll forever hold dear

DEEP LOVE

Love. . .
It's giving your last
To help someone else get pass
Their hunger
Their misfortune
With a part of your portion
That God has blessed you with
Not questioning why, how or what if
Love. . .

Love. . .
It's taking the time to smile
Going the extra mile
Bringing joy to others
As we uplift our sisters and brothers
Understanding it's not only about you
Only what God wants you to do
Love. . .

Love. . .
It's looking at your son
And realizing he's the one
That you have to hand over to die
For sins and other countless lies
That he never did
But you want the people to live
Love. . .
It doesn't get any deeper than that

GIVING

Take my tithes Lord and bless it
Because I give in faith.

Take my offering Lord and bless it
I give both with a smile on my face.

My first fruits, 10%
And anything extra I want to give.

May it bless this church
And prosper me as I live.

I am your obedient servant
And I do as you command.

I acknowledge you as my faithful high priest
As I lift up my hands.

JESUS

Jesus
Yes that name
We thank you Lord for forgiving us
Putting up with our fuss

Jesus
Yes you Lord
The one who provides comfort and healing
Your love is such a great feeling

Jesus
Such a sweet sound
We honor you, we worship you
We give you praise
With no limits or bounds

My sweet Jesus
Yes you're mine
I'm so proud to say
Looking forward to your coming
Looking forward to the day

Jesus
Yes Jesus
I love you
You have brought me through
I give you honor in all I do

Jesus
Love you Jesus

My sweet Jesus
Mine, mine, mine

Jesus
I love you

COME TO CHURCH

I can't!
I have hated my brother,
Lied to my mother,
Caused pain to so many,
I'm not worth a single penny.
"But God is forgiving,
Come to church!"

I can't!
I've never read the word,
The songs I've never heard,
I don't know how to pray,
I'm confused with all they say.
"But God is a teacher,
Come to church!"

I can't!
I have pain in my head,
I'm too weak to get out of bed,
I won't be able to stand,
There's no hope,
You really don't understand.
"But God is a healer,
Come to church!"

I can't!
No one likes me,
I want to die,
I have no relationships
And love passes me by,
Daily I'm miserable, daily I cry,
To see another day,
All I ask is why?
"But God loves you,
Come to church!"

Your influence is good,
These things I didn't know.
I'm curious about this God,

With you I will go,
To know. . .this God who will
Forgive me, teach me, heal me and love me.
"With you God is well pleased,
Now let's go to church."

I'M REACHING

Lord, I come before you
With outstretched hands
For you to forgive me
Is my only demand
I want to be born again
I want my sinful ways to end
I want to mirror your love
Your walk
I want to change
My views, my heart, my talk
How wonderful it is
To finally know your name
I desire life everlasting
My spirit is
No longer the same
I'm reaching out to you
Giving you my all
Forgive me; shower me with your love
And pick me up from my fall

GET YOUR HEAVEN ON

No it ain't cool
To act like a fool
Disobey the Lord's rules
Be a number in the devil's pool
Be a Christian diva
A Jesus Christ soldier
Don't let nobody hold ya
Back from God's will
Because His love is real
Don't let nobody steal
Your joy, your love, your integrity
Rebuke the devil and let your soul be free
And get your heaven on
I get my heaven on
Get your heaven on
Your heaven on

First you have to accept
that Jesus died and paid a debt
that was yours
that was mine
we were way outta line
with God's word
His instructions
Now get on your knees and speak your confessions
Repent your sins
Let the Lord in
It's a new day
Let your new life begin
And get your heaven on
I get my heaven on
Get your heaven on
Your heaven on

Open your mouth
Shout to Him your praise
With your hands you raise
Him up
For all the ways

He protected you
Loved you
Brought you through
All the pain
And now you gain
His mercy
His favor
He now knows your name
So get your heaven on
I get my heaven on
Get your heaven on
Your heaven on

FORGIVE

Your husband had a baby
By another lady
Now you're crying tears
Thinking all the wasted years
Who is this man you thought you knew
Having a secret lover he lied to you
Now he had the nerve to apologize
So ashamed he can't look you in your eyes
Says he didn't mean it
It was a big mistake
You look to God
How much more do I have to take
But I know it's hard the pain you had to hide
You held it all in
You cried and cried
But you have to forgive
You have to forgive so that you can live
You don't want to hold on to all he did
You have to forgive
God wants you to live
Forgive

Your child was murdered
You have to identify the body
You're full of rage
Wondering how can anybody
Kill your child
Do such a sin
You hate that person
All you want is revenge
As you go to bed
Evil thoughts run through your head
Your family fell apart
Cause you've had a change of heart
You spend all your time thinking what you're gonna do
To this evil person that really hurt you
You hate them
You want their life to end
But I know it's hard the pain you had to hide

You held it all in
You cried and cried
But you have to forgive
You have to forgive so that you can live
He'll take care of what they did
You have to forgive
God wants you to live
Forgive

Your father was abusive
He treated you bad
He said you were the child
He wished he never had
You went out of your way
To try to please him
No matter what you did
He wouldn't give in
He wanted you out of his sight
You constantly had to fight
This went on for so long
You're thinking what's the problem
What is going on
You didn't know what call it
Your mother said he was an alcoholic
The damage is done
You hate him so much
You don't care for his love
Or even his touch
But I know it's hard
The pain you had to hide
You held it all in
You cried and cried
But you have to forgive
You have to forgive so that you can live
He had a sickness
He doesn't know what he did
You have to forgive
God wants you to live
Forgive
So that you can live
You have to forgive

HIS LOVE, TRY IT

His love has opened my heart,
Took away anger and dried my tears.
His love has removed worry,
Washed away pain as well as fear.
His love has given me favor at work,
Removed my debt and made me financially stable.
His love has changed me; made me stronger,
Without Him I am not capable.
His love is amazing.
Words can give it no justice
And to compare would take a lifetime.
His love,
The only true love
Is awesome.
You should try it sometime.

DID YOU KNOW

Did you know that God is almighty, amazing
And full of love too?
Did you know that God gave His son
As a sacrifice for you?
Did you know that you can speak to Him anytime
Day or night?
Did you know that you cannot hide from Him
You're always in His sight?
Did you know He forgives all sins
Big or small?
Did you know He loves you even when you ignore Him,
Curse Him, blame Him through it all?
Did you know that He comforts
And heals?
Did you know that evil exists
And the devil is real?
Did you know He will protect you
Through all strife?
Did you know that once you receive Him
You could have eternal life?
Did you?
If you don't know
Now you know.
Read your bible
It will tell you so.

HE ALWAYS HELPS

As I walk
He makes a path for me to follow
When I try to grab on to things
He takes harmful things out of my reach
If I fall into a pit of problems
He removes them causing them to become shallow
When I abuse my tongue
He takes away my voice and corrects my speech
When evil thoughts invade my mind
He feels my head with His love and kindness
If I start looking for insight from the wrong people
He takes them out of my vision
When I feel like I'm about to explode with anger
He fills my spirit with peace and soundness
Throughout life and all of these ups and downs
He's always there to help me make a decision
God, my helper

MOTIVATE ME

My mind is going crazy
I'm so confused
What direction should I take
With life there are no rules
My kids are demanding
Work is never ending
Problems are constant
I don't know whether
My life is beginning or ending
My mental state is questionable
Am I going crazy
Lord help me out
Give me the strength
With you I've become lazy
I'm giving you my hand
Handing over my soul
Restore my spirit
I desire to become whole
In you
With you
By you
For you
Motivate me Lord
Motivate me Lord
Motivate me
I love you

GOD'S LOVE

Tears of joy
now replace tears of sadness
Happiness is more constant
than the madness
Faith has taken away
my sorrow
I no longer look at the past
and look forward to tomorrow
"this is what God's love has done for me"

I live by truth
No longer by lies
I look to Him for everything
When I used to close my eyes
Love in my heart
Has now replaced my soulless pain
I now feel worth
When I used to feel lost and drained
"this is what God's love has done for me"

I now forgive
And no longer hold a grudge
I take people for who they are
I'm no longer quick to judge
I give more of myself
Without worrying about receiving
I used to look to the world
But that joy was deceiving
"this is what God's love has done for me"

As my Father loved me
Still loves me
No matter what I've gone through
I too have unconditional love
With no limits or bounds
For you
This is what God's love has done for me
And for you

REFLECT GOD'S LOVE

There is no love greater than God's
His love is so wonderful that you or I could never comprehend
He loves us so much that He gave His son for a living sacrifice
So that our life could begin
And now we've become so mighty that we want to disrespect Him
And forget His presence
We've gone so far as to take the word "Christ" out of Christmas
We're losing ourselves
Believe me there will be consequences
If we're not strong and able to endure
the church too will fall apart
Link arms with the person beside you
This is the way to conquer evil
United as one
Strong in heart
It is our duty to spread His word
Show His goodness
And speak His name
Our reflection of His love will soon become attractive
and they too will want the same

HE MOTIVATES ME

I'm able to get through trials,
Through tribulations.
I'm able to face the world
With all its complications.
Nothing can defeat me
Because the Lord motivates me.

Pain may come
But I know healing is on the way.
Tears may fall
But I know joy will occur the same day.
Nothing can hurt me
Because the Lord motivates me.

Evil will lurk
And try to change my heart.
Evil will challenge me.
Try to tear my soul apart.
Nothing can damage me
Because the Lord motivates me.

I don't fit into your groups
Because I'm part of God's click.
I don't adapt to your ways.
I only desire to be the one that God picks.
Nothing can change me
Because the Lord motivates me.

You cannot defeat me!
You cannot hurt me!
You cannot damage me!
You cannot change me!
Because the Lord motivates me!

STILL I PUT YOUR FIRST

Frustrated with
life,
work,
people,
school,
relationships. . .
but still I reach out to you, talk to you, pray to you.
Lord I put you first with all that I do
and frustration changes to encouragement.

Angry with
my spouse,
my kids,
family,
my friends,
the world. . .
but still I reach out to you, talk to you, pray to you.
Lord I put your first with all that I do
and anger changes to happiness.

Confused about
war,
unkindness,
hatred,
love,
decisions. . .
but still I reach out to you, talk to you, pray to you.
Lord I put your first with all that I do
and confusion changes to understanding.

Fear of
the future,
the unknown,
the challenge,
failing,
consequences. . .

but still I reach out to you, talk to you, pray to you.
Lord I put you first with all that I do
and fear changes to courage.

I will always put your first with all that I do.

YOU MY LORD

You are wonderful
You are amazing
This you have shown
My love for you
Your love for me
Has definitely grown
How you could be doubted
How you could be mistreated
Truly blows my mind
You've been my guide
Been my comforter
You're with me all the time
For loving me
For forgiving me
For carrying me
I thank you
For believing in me
For touching my heart
For dying for me
I love you
My Lord

IN THE NAME OF JESUS

When people bring you down
And make you mad
When friends abandon you
And you feel they're all you had
When loneliness grips you
And you think you don't fit in
Just reach out your hands
And give it to Him
"in the name of Jesus"

You're decisions in life
May have changed your plans
You counted on your mate to guide you
Or take your hand
You've given up hope
Don't know where to begin
Just reach out your hands
And give it to Him
"in the name of Jesus"

You've done things in your past
That now gives you shame
Hate and anger was so visible
That people cringed at the sound of your name
Now you feel you're unworthy of forgiveness
Because of what you did then
Just reach out your hands
And give it to Him
"in the name of Jesus"

The devil is tricky
And will pull at your soul
He will lead you astray and confuse you
This is his goal
If you start feeling weak
And desire to live in sin
Just reach out your hands
And give it to Him
"in the name of Jesus"

THE LORD HAS AUTHORITY

My first husband was verbally abusive,
My second husband was abusive with his hands,
My boyfriend was an alcoholic,
I always thought I needed a man.
No more!
I am a great woman spiritually.
Only the Lord has authority over me.

I'm worried that I will never get out of debt,
I think I may lose my job.
Fear from reading the paper or watching the news
Has me cautious of disease, the weather or being robbed.
No more!
I am a great woman spiritually.
Only the Lord has authority over me.

My husband is very demanding,
My children crave attention,
I desire the perfect appearance or body
Because I don't want to lose my man's affection.
No more!
I am a great woman spiritually.
Only the Lord has authority over me.

I thought being rich would fix my problems.
I thought if I altered my body I would attain fame.
I thought the most important thing in life was to be known by the world,
Not knowing it was more important to believe in the Lord and praise His name.
No more!
I am a great woman spiritually.
Only the Lord has authority over me.

GOD WILL FORGIVE

The lies you told
The adultery of your past
Your heart that was once so cold
The bad way you received money that didn't last
God will forgive
Because God is love

All the times you've cheated
The temptation you once played a role
All the people you mistreated
The things you've stole
God will forgive
Because God is love

Don't let your past discourage you
From letting him in your heart
Put God first in all that you do
And for this He'll give you a new start
God will forgive
Because God is love

BECAUSE OF YOU

Because of you I know who Christ is
As a result I hold Him in my heart
Because of you I am reborn
As a result I am a new person
Because of you I have learned new things
As a result I now spread this knowledge
Because of you I now show Him praise
As a result I constantly worship His name
Because of you my spirit it stronger
As a result I'm finally on the right path
I no longer worry and joy overrides all negativity
And I thank you

CONCENTRATE ON ME

You feel the world is against you.
Who is on your side?
You've tried to find the answer,
You've tried to find the end to your struggle.
You tried and tried.
But God says,
your sadness I'll take and in return here's joy.
With joy you shall be fulfilled.
Scream and I'll relax you.
Cry and I'll take away your tears.
Just stand still.
You want to die?
No! I'm not ready to bring you home
Because your life has meaning
And your purpose is to worship me.
With every step you're not alone.
I'm always by your side.
When the world's against you it's also against me.
Just hold my hand and let me guide you.
With me you can't go wrong.
You will trample evil; your struggles will vanish.
As my child you will be strong.
Don't worry about the world, just concentrate on me.
Their fate will soon come.
Pain will come hard, the terror will be fierce
And the love that I was offering they'll wish they had some.

GIVE HIM SOME PRAISE

I'm not perfect
You're not perfect
And He loves us anyway
We turn our love for Him on and off
But His love continues every day
We ignore Him
But He still listens to our prayers
When we're lost we don't look to Him
But when we're in need He's always there
Isn't God awesome
Clap your hands and give Him some praise

You throw tantrums because He's not on your schedule
But He still gives you what you desire
Outwardly you're beautiful but your thoughts are evil
And continuously he fights to keep you out of the fire
You say left but He's telling you right
You say no when He says yes
Even through your confusion
He still gives you His best
Isn't God awesome
Clap your hands and give Him some praise

When you think He doesn't know He knows
When you do wrong He will tell you so
When you feel lost believe me your already found
When you're lonely you can be assured He's always around
I shouldn't have to ask you if God is awesome
Stand up
Clap your hands
Shout out and give Him some praise

HOPE YOU'RE SCARED

Envy, greed, jealousy and lust
To avoid these things
Jesus is a must
Don't put your heart in the world and possessions
Give it to the Lord
With all your confessions
Don't reach out for what she has
Grab on to the Lord
Don't mimic his life
His way
Copy the Lord
There's no need to be jealous
Because God has individual plans for all in His book
He doesn't care about your fancy cars
How much money you have
Or your looks
He has tunnel vision directed at your soul
Is it dirty, broken, fallen apart or whole
Do you recognize His purpose
Do you know His name
Have you been wearing a mask
Just going through the motions
Playing games
Time is short
His return is coming
I hope you're prepared
For those left behind there will be
Pain, torture, devastation, terror
I hope that you are scared
The truth is if you don't know the Lord
Your mind will be lost
Your soul confused
Today take Him in your heart
Reclaim your soul
And let the world know it's Him you choose

GOD IS AWESOME

God is awesome
I said God is awesome and his presence is real
I am a witness
I am a believer
I'm telling you His love is surreal
He is my king
My comforter
My everything
and I just want you to know
All you have to do is reach out to Him
And you too shall grow
Lift up your hands and let Him in
Tell Him you believe
Ask Him to forgive your sins
You think your sins are too big
No
there's none of that
All you have to do is believe
Bow your head and drop to your knees
Father I love you
Please forgive my sins
Reclaim my soul
To walk, talk and breathe in your way
Is my goal
Thank you Father
Please allow my shine to radiate so that all can see
That your grace and glory now runs through me
Thank you Father
It's just that simple
Not difficult at all
Just reach out to Him
And give Him a call
I'm telling you
God is awesome and His presence is real
Become a witness
Become a believer
And you too will see that His love is surreal

TURN ON THE LIGHTS

I blindly walked through darkness
Facing the same obstacles
Not knowing where to turn
Unable to dodge the incoming evils
But I felt secure
No one could see my faults
Witness my sins
See the tears that constantly fell from my eyes
Little did I know my safe haven
Was really torture
Deteriorating my soul
My faith was dwindling
I was losing sight for Him
For my life I needed to take a hold
So I decided to switch on that light
And reborn were my eyes
My soul open
My direction appeared so clearly
For His light was my guide
The tears are gone
And my faith is renewed
All that I am is visible to all
Because I have no shame
I now live the Christian way
And evil is blinded by my shine
When darkness starts creeping
Turn on the light
Of His love
And allow him to guide you through

I DON'T KNOW YOU

I was reaching out to you
But you wouldn't hold on
I showed you the answers
But your eyes were always closed
I tried to give you encouragement
But your head was bent down in shame
I was giving you direction
But you kept taking wrong turns
I tried to teach you patience
But you were always in a rush
I sent you friends with loving hearts and souls
But you desired ones full of anger and hate
I opened your ears to hear my name
But you ignored me
Now I don't know you
All you had to do was
Hold on
Open your eyes
Lift your head
Stay on the path
Be still
And know my name

I WILL UPLIFT

Come to me with your problems
Come to me with your fears
I have your answers
I'll dry your tears
There is no other
Who can love you like I do
There is no other
Who will stay by your side with all you go through
You are my children
Such special gifts
Come to me even when you're down
I will uplift

FATHER YOU ARE WORTHY

Dear Lord,
Please lay your hands upon me.
Give me the strength to get through this ordeal.
My mind is wandering, the pain is unbearable,
I need you to help me be still.
I tried to fix the damage myself
But now I'm giving it to you.
Have mercy on me Father,
Heal me, ease my mind.
I know only you can. . .I really do.
I feel your presence; I know you're by my side,
I can feel your wonderful touch.
Thank you Father,
You are so worthy.
I love you, thank you so much.

DEVIL LAST

I know what I did in the past
I know how I used to be
I don't need you to remind me
So look at yourself before you scrutinize me
I serve a forgiving God
Who has washed away my sins
I serve a loving God
Who loves me now
He even loved me then
I no longer look to the world
And I don't worry about the rest
If you're trying to keep me down
Please don't hold your breath
I'm looking forward
Not looking to the past
I'm putting God first
And the devil last

SHOUT AMEN

The Lord has been good to me!
Has He been good to you?
I said the Lord has been good to me!
If He's been good to you shout Amen!

When I looked to my friends to solve my problems
They weren't always there,
But when I started talking to Jesus He was always near.
If the Lord has been good to you
Shout Amen!

When I was living in sin and tried to change
People wouldn't forget and trashed my name,
But the Lord said my sins are forgiven
And no matter what He still loves me just the same.
If the Lord has been good to you
Shout Amen!

Sometimes the tears fall, I have pain in my heart,
And comfort is hard to find,
But the Lord eases my pain, lets me feel his presence
And tells me that He's there all the time.
If the Lord has been good to you
Shout Amen!

When I was doing worldly things I was lost, confused
And didn't know what decisions to make,
But the Lord took my hand, showed me how to share His word,
And guided me to the right paths to take.
If the Lord has been good to you
Shout Amen!

When I feel alone He tells me I'm wrong,
When I'm weak He makes me strong,
When I'm sad He puts joy in my heart,
When I hit a dead end He gives me a new start,

When evil lurks He makes them my footstool,
And when peer pressure starts tugging He reminds me that loving him is only cool.

I know the Lord has been good to me.
If he's been good to you shout Amen!

PRAISE YOUR NAME

Lord let the melody from these instruments
Flow in your name
The beating of the drums
The strumming of the strings
Tapping of the keys
Let it flow Lord
As we praise your name

Lord as we move to the rhythm
Swaying our hips
Clapping our hands
Tapping our feet
To the many sounds
Help us feel the beat
As we praise your name

Lord help our voices to rise as a whole
Let the sounds flow
From our mouths
And words spoken from our bodies
Help us penetrate souls
As we praise your name

Yes Lord!
Today we sing
Today we dance
Today we play
As we praise and worship
Your holy name

FORGIVING GOD

Lord, how can I come to you when I'm full of sin?
I don't know the songs, can't memorize scriptures and pray. . .
I don't know where to begin.
My past is full of wrong and I didn't care about others,
Nor did I follow your commandment of honor your father and mother.
And love. . .well loving was just something that I couldn't do.
I was disappointed in everyone. . .
Even you.

Lord, how can I come to you when my life isn't right?
I sell and do drugs and every other day I'm in some type of fight.
I've been in and out of rehab, been in and out of jail.
People don't know whether I'm coming or going.
Shoot, I can't even tell.
There's no hope for me.
I feel there's nothing left for me to do.
I have disappointed everyone and I know that includes you.

Lord, how can I come to you when I've lost my way?
I haven't read the bible in years and forgot how to pray.
I placed you behind me because I felt my prayers were ignored.
The devil was hitting me left and right and knocking at my door.
I had to fix things my way, on my time. . .did what I had to do.
I was impatient, selfish and I didn't want to wait for you.

Dear children, didn't I say come as you are?
Don't you know what that means?
When you come in my presence dirty you will leave clean.
All you have to have is faith and believe in me.
Understand that no one is perfect but your Lord God. . .me!
From this point on take steps forward, leave your past behind.
Start reading my word and you will grow spiritually in due time.
Your love will soon mirror the love I have for you.
My presence in your life will radiate with all that you do.
There are no excuses not to praise me.
There are no reasons not to worship me.

You don't have to come new.
I'm a forgiving God.
I forgive all.
And this includes you.

DON'T LOSE YOUR GRIP

The devil will tell you
That you are no good
That your life is not worth living
He'll say
Go ahead
Do that sin

Hold on to God's word child
Don't lose your grip

The world will tell you
That you have to look a certain way
The world will keep you down
Just by the evil things that are going on
People will try to change your heart
Make you lose your mind

Hold on to God's love child
Don't lose your grip

So called friends
Will try to change your view
False teachers
Will lead you down the wrong path
New and incorrect religions
Will become plenty
Many people will claim to be Jesus

Hold on to God's hand
Don't lose your grip
God's the only way

I LOVE, NEED AND WANT YOU LORD

I love you, I love you, I love you Lord. . .
You are so wonderful,
You are so grand,
You helped me see
I know you understand.

I need you, I need you, I need you Lord. . .
You guide my steps,
You shield my heart,
You hold my hand,
Without you I would fall apart.

I want you, I want you, I want you Lord. . .
To use me in your way,
To help me bring in more,
I want to spread your word,
Because I love you Lord.

ALL IN YOUR NAME

We kneel in worship
And praise without shame

We sing songs to you
And shout your name

We read the bible
And study your word

We listen to our teachers
And share what was heard

You have our hearts Lord
No one else could compete

You have our love Lord
It's yours to forever keep

CAN'T BE BORROWED

Wash me Lord
Cleanse my soul

Touch me Lord
Make me whole

Hold my hand
Open my mind

Help me to look to the future
Keep my past behind

I love you Lord
Today. . .tomorrow

Your love cannot be
Stolen
Bought
Or borrowed

HELP LORD

Hold my hand Lord and lead my way,
There's another mountain called turmoil that I have to climb today.
Lift me up Lord, let me feel the wind in my hair,
There's a big pothole in my path and it's called despair.
Hold me tight Lord because I'm being pulled here and there,
I'm being faced with difficult decisions and it's just not fair.

Give me strength Lord and open my heart,
There's a wall of ice called forgiveness but my anger is slowly breaking it apart.
Lend me your eyes Lord so that I may see the right path to your heavenly place,
There's an evil being called the devil always blocking my way
And his goal is to stop me from seeing your face.

YOUR WILL IS MY WAY

When you're feeling discouraged and don't know where to begin,
When bad things come at you daily
And you don't know when it's going to end.
Give it to the Lord and pray,
"Lord, today and everyday let your will be my way."

When you speak and feel no one listens,
When that joyful spirit you once had is missing,
Give it to the Lord and pray,
"Lord, today and everyday let your will be my way."

When the tears fall and never seem to stop,
When you try to hold on to love that always seems to drop,
Give it to the Lord and pray,
"Lord, today and everyday let your will be my way."

When you have to make difficult decisions
And end up making mistakes,
When the pressures of the world ride you
And you can't seem to get a break,
Give it to the Lord and pray,
"Lord, today and everyday let your will be my way."

NO LONGER WORRIED

You can't bring me down
Because I have God on my side.
He's my strength, healer, comforter. . .
My one and only guide.
Your words of despair,
I put them over there.
They're no longer stored in my heart
To cause me despair.

With God I am strong.
With Him I walk on solid ground.
If you left tomorrow it wouldn't bother me,
It's Him I want to keep around.
I forgive you for the pain you've caused me,
I still love you no doubt,
But now that I feel and know the love of God
Those things I no longer worry about.

DIED FOR US

We cheated
We lied
He forgave
He died

Full of hatred
Full of pride
He forgave
He died

Didn't listen
Didn't confide
He forgave
He died

Didn't follow
Not by his side
He forgave
He died

Lived in sin
Tried to hide
He forgave
He died

For us

RECLAIM MY SOUL

Has your heart been opened?
Has your soul been saved?
Do you now understand
The life that He gave?
He died for me.
He died for you.
He died for us all.
He's always there for you,
All you have to do is reach out and give Him a call.
Lord, I love you!
I believe. . .please reclaim my soul.
Wash me Lord,
Please make me whole.
Forgive my sins.
I lay them before you forever. . .starting today.
I stand before you now,
Reaching out lifting my hands as I pray.

I now see that there is no other God but you.
I now see that you are kind, forgive sins. . .so true.
I now know that I'm never alone, you're always by my side.
I now understand that the paths will never by scary with you as my guide.
I now acknowledge that you are capable of opening many, many doors.
I'm giving you my all
Reclaim my soul Lord. . .
It's yours.

Chapter 2

"Family, Friends & All"

FAMILY AND FRIENDS

This is our family
These are our friends
United spiritually
Bonded with love for one another
Parents, grandparents,
Aunts, uncles, cousins,
Sisters and brothers
And friends
Yes
them too
We don't share blood
But were bonded by heart
And it's beautiful
As it also should be for you
This unity should be shared
With the younger generation
We as adults have to set the tone
Build the foundation
Knowledge
Teach it
God
Preach it
Love
Show it
Pain
Comfort it
Help
Provide it
And anger
Forgive it
Set the example
And they too shall grow
A reflection of our image
Through them shall show
The love of God
Unity
Strength

And family love
Let's bring back what family and friends
Are really made of

SIS, WE DON'T

Sis, we don't talk much but I see
How you're taking care of
Your house
Your children
Your husband
And I'm proud of you

Sis, we don't talk much but I know
You have grown into a woman
Full of strength
Confidence
Love
And I'm proud of you

Sis, we don't talk much but I hear
That you're prospering
In life
Your marriage
Your job
And I'm proud of you

Keep growing, prospering and taking care of your family
Because I'm proud of you

MOM

I watched you wipe away tears,
Bandage wounds,
I listened to your comforting words
And remember you singing uplifting tunes.
My children now get the same from me,
You have stamped your
"**M**arking **O**n **M**e."

I watched you love dad
And saw the joy in his eyes.
I listened to the way you communicated,
Supported one another. . .always side by side.
My husband now gets the same from me,
You have stamped your
"**M**arking **O**n **M**e!"

I watched you worship Jesus and honor our Father;
His word you obeyed.
I listened to you pray and have conversation with Him
As you kept Him near to you every day.
My Father now gets the same from me,
You have stamped your
"**M**arking **O**n **M**e!"

THAT ONE

Every day we look for that one;
That one to make us smile;
That one who can lift you up;
That one who talks to you for a while;
That one who tells you to never give up;
That one who offers a hand;
That one who gives without looking for a return;
That one who truly understands;
That one that shows a kindness
That is a gift and not learned.
Thank you for being that one.

HAPPY BIRTHDAY TO YOU

Smile
Clap
Rejoice as you move
Celebrate your birth
How you've improved
From a twinkle in your mother's eye
To joy by your husband's side
Your children look up to you
Friends adore you
Happy birthday
Happy birthday to you

You've cried
You've laughed
But you've seen another year
You fell
And you got up
You defeated all fear
Your strength takes you higher
Knowledge makes you wiser
Happy birthday
Happy birthday to you

Through your heart
Your words
Your walk
Pure character is shown
Your faith alone
Shows how you've grown
Naturally
Spiritually
Perfected love
Perfected beauty
Happy birthday
Happy birthday to you

HUSBAND, THANK YOU

Thank you
for being the father
that you are to our children
the way you love them
care for them
care for us
we love you

Thank you
for taking care of home
providing security
providing order
providing comfort
we love you

Thank you
for your support
your time
your love & energy
we appreciate it
appreciate you

IN YOU WE SEE

A true man of strength
That is what we've seen
To us things may look tough
But you always say
It's not what it seems
Through sickness
You still stand tall
Throughout the worst situations
You allow no one to fall
You are an extraordinary man
And for this we love you

A true man of God
This you definitely show
You've taught many of us
And helped us spiritually grow
Faithfully you read your bible
And share what you've learned
We see God blessing you abundantly
For this we too yearn
You are an extremely faithful man
And for this we love you

A true man of caring
You show this every time we're near
Whether it's through laughter
A hug
Or consoling us through tears
You reassure us that love is everlasting and forgiving
Love nurtures life
You demonstrate this daily
Through the love you have for your wife
You are a passionate and loving man
And for this we love you

In you we see
An extraordinary, faithful and loving man
And for this
We will always, always love you

GETTING MARRIED

We've been friends for many, many years.
We've shared laughter, shared joy
As well as tears.
And now this moment. . .
You're getting married.
Wow!
I can't think of a moment I've seen you happier
Than you are now.
And I'm proud of you.
No one is more deserving of the love that you are receiving.
I pray that it will continually grow
And you'll allow God to do all the leading.
As you go on to your new journey
And this new chapter in your life begins,
Always remember that I'm here for you,
I will always have your back
As your sistergirl, sisterfriend.

OUR FAMILY

We are a family. . .
That gives without receiving
Not about failure but all about achieving
When wrong we'll make it right
With no lose chains, we'll always remain tight
We worship God, yes together we pray
We do what we mean and mean what we say
We have a very strong foundation
Within this family
Past, present and soon to be

WE ARE A FAMILY

We are a family that prays together
We are a family who worships God and no other
We are a family who walks a righteous path
We are a family who shares pain, love and a good laugh
We are a family who provides a strong hand when in need
We are a family who shares their worth without a lot of greed
This is the foundation of our family
Past, present and soon to be

GODPARENT'S LOVE

As a little girl to a grown woman
We'll teach the way
Of life, love, beauty, kindness
And how to pray
Your tears we'll wipe away
Your hand we'll hold
Your dreams we'll back them
And support all your goals
God's word we'll teach you
And pray by your side
Living by example
We'll be your guide
This is our promise to you
As long as we live
A godmother's love
Is what we'll provide, share and give

As a little girl to a grown woman
We'll lead you in your way
Of respect, strength, prosperity and love
With God leading you day by day
Your fears we'll comfort
When you fall we'll lift you up
Your thoughts we'll listen
We'll always encourage you and won't let you give up
We'll teach you about God
And how Jesus died for our sins
We'll make sure you understand
That all things are possible with Him
This is our promise to you
As long as we live
A godfather's love
Is what we'll provide, share and give

I THANK YOU

Nine months of care
Hearing your voice
Feeling your touch
Then you gave me life
And I thank you

Nursed my wounds
Knowledge of the world
Visions of new things
My child life was so beautiful
And I thank you

Still you provide wisdom
A shoulder
A hand
Your heart
The only way that a mother could
And I thank you

FATHER

Father you are a great man in my eyes

Always there when we need you to listen, comfort and guide

Today I follow your footsteps learning as I go

Hoping that God will bless me with your ways as I grow

Everyone you encounter enjoys you as much as us

Remember on this day and forever that you are loved so much

SON

So proud I am to have you as my child, you're such a special one

Openly kind, very intelligent, spirit filled you are and your life has just begun

No one could replace you or make me love them as much as I do
you. . .my sweet son

THANK GOD FOR YOU

Your words have lifted me up and changed my ways.
I have grown spiritually and now give the Lord all my praise.
I tell you this because I want you to know that
You are appreciated and adored.
Your words, trust and honesty have touched me and so many more.
Keep doing what you do because you are making changes in this world
More than you know.
I believe that all that you've started will grow and grow.
I also know I have truly been blessed when I met you.
You're a good friend.
I love you
And thank God for you.

TRUE MAN OF GOD

You've been an inspiration to so many
For so many years.
From spreading the word, listening to confessions
And wiping away tears.
You are a true man of God
Dedicated to His word as it is in the bible.
No matter what time of day or what you were doing
If you were needed then you were there. . .yes you are my idol.
As you retire and follow this new path in life
We pray that you'll receive an abundance of blessings like you've witnessed through us.
We've been blessed to have you as a father, a pastor and a friend.
We hope that you realize that you are loved so much.

LOVED YOU FROM THE BEGINNING

From the first moment I felt you inside me
I loved you
You were a joy to watch grow, play
And do things so innocently
Now you are a woman
Whose steps do not falter
Whose voice is not unheard
Who has a heart which you give with no boundaries
And hands which you lend
To those in need
You've made me happy from the beginning
And I'm proud of what you have accomplished
I look forward to the future of loving you more
Today, tomorrow. . .forever

IN YOUR FOOTSTEPS

To walk in your footsteps
Would give me honor and pride
The way you keep this family together
Could never be denied
Showing our mother love
And providing her a helping hand
Helping us with our homework
And showing us you understand
Bringing food to the table
And keeping a roof over our heads
Kneeling beside us as we pray
Tucking us into our beds

You've showed me how a strong and devoted man
Can make it in this world today
By keeping your head up, striving for more
And never letting adversities get in your way
You're my father
And one day I hope to be just like you
When I have children
I pray they look at me and feel the same way too

YOU ARE ALSO NEEDED

Today children are faced with obstacles
That we never went through.
They need guidance, attention, love
And the knowledge of God too.
The presence of a man is undeniably needed in their life
And in their heart.
A mother's love is expected
But your role as a friend, brother, husband or father
Also plays a big part.
Show them that you were created
To lead and guide them the right way.
They will learn through your examples
As they follow and watch what you say.
Show them that a man's display of emotions
Isn't a sign of weakness.
Tell them that if they are always true with themselves
They will always feel completeness.
Teach them mental strength in your ability
To be respectful, honest and understanding.
Hold their hand and be there for them
And let them know your love is undemanding.
With all of this
Acknowledge God in your life
And they will do the same.
We love you all not only on Father's Day
And we honor your name.

SISTERGIRL, SISTERFRIEND

We met through our significant others
Right away we seemed to bond
Unaware of the friendship that was forming
Unaware that God was waving His holy wand
Little did we know our sisterhood was about to begin
I love you and thank you for being
My sistergirl
My sisterfriend

Tears have been shed
Comfort has been provided
Discussions have been deep
Our thoughts sometimes divided
A hug given
A prayer shared
Often helped the heart to mend
I often think
What would I do without
My sistergirl
My sisterfriend

To have you in my life as a dear, dear friend
I've truly been blessed
To inherit sisters without a bloodline
Who would have guessed
I want you to understand that there's no one in the world better
That he could send
To be
My sistergirl
My sisterfriend

BEAUTIFUL YOU ARE

You give without wanting
You share without receiving
You love unconditionally
And your heart has no boundaries
Beautiful you are and we love you

This family is your core
You are the binding link
And strong is your grasp
You've been there for each and every one of us
Beautiful you are and we love you

You are a strong woman of God
Your steps do not falter
And your spirit glows
You radiate and shine with your love for only Him
Beautiful you are and we love you

We all appreciate you
We all admire and adore your strength
No one in life could ever replace you
And we hope today that we show you how
Beautiful you are
And that we love you

MOTHER AND BEST FRIEND

Mom, I hope you realize how much I appreciate you.
No matter what my circumstances I can always count on you.
When my world was coming to an end you were there
To wipe the tears from my eyes.
When I was lost and didn't know what direction to take
You were my guide.
When I thought hope was forbidden
You gave me reassurance.
When I made the wrong decisions
You never laughed at my ignorance.
The many times that I wanted to quit
You said that option wasn't a choice.
When I have been at a loss of words
I could always count on you to be my voice.

For these reasons and so many more
I will always look up to you.
You're my mother, my best friend
And I love you.

MOTHER

My mother, a strong woman indeed

Open are her arms to every need

True in spirit, soul and mind

Heart of gold, smile that shines

Ever so joyful, thoughtful and full of love

Remarkable woman sent from up above

DAUGHTER

Definitely a blessing when God gave you to me

A beautiful child, now a woman so lovely

Unique is your kindness with a joyful personality

Great love is what you give to yourself and others unselfishly

Hope the joy you've given me you too receive as a mother

Truly you are one of a kind and I would ask for no other

Eloquent lady and a respected woman with a strong mind

Remarkable you are this daughter of mine

LOVE OF MY MOTHER

I watch her walk and I see
Confidence in her steps.
I look at her smile and I see
Joy that cannot be replaced.
I listen to her words and I hear
A truth that no one can forget.
I see wisdom in her eyes and a warmth
That can only be obtained from her embrace.

The Lord died for our sins showing the
Ultimate sign of love for us.
A love that could never be duplicated
Or matched by no other,
And it's continuous no matter how much
You disobey or fuss.
He has given me the next best thing which is so similar. . .
The love of my mother.

SOMEONE TO COUNT ON

A shoulder to lean on,
A helping hand,
A voice of encouragement,
A mind to understand.

Always by your side,
Forever on your mind,
Always in your corner,
Forever one of a kind.

Someone to count on,
Someone who's always there,
Someone who will always be with you,
Someone to care. . .
Mom, I love you.

LOVE OF A MOTHER

The love of a mother,
There's nothing else like it.
It's so pure that no matter where you are,
You'll always feel it.
When no one is there to lift you up
She gives you a hand.
When no one else can comprehend
She always understands.
When you feel your world is coming to an end
She brings it back together.
When everyone else deserts you
She's by your side forever.
When you have doubt
She will reassure you.
When the tears constantly fall
She will comfort you.

Her strength has made you strong,
Her honesty will allow you to do no wrong,
Her knowledge has made you smarter,
Her determination makes you work harder,
Her teachings have made you wise,
Her wisdom has opened your eyes,
Her attention has made you listen to what others say,
Her walk with God has increased your faith.

For these reasons alone we should all say,
Mother's we love you. . .Happy Mother's Day.

SUCH STRONG BLACK WOMEN MOST DEFINITELY

When we were growing up
So hard were the times.
We didn't have a dollar to our name
Let alone a dime.
But no matter what
You were always there.
To bandage a wound,
To wipe away a tear.
You even showered us with love
When we were in need.
My mother,
Such a strong black woman, most definitely.

You set us on the right path
And taught us how to maintain.
You said no matter how successful we become
Don't forget from where you came.
You catered to our wants
Before you thought about your own.
You taught us about the Lord
And how He never leaves us alone.
So when I think who in this world
Is the most special to me,
It has to be my mother,
Such a strong black woman, most definitely.

From a child to a woman
You've been by my side.
Everything that you taught me
Has given me confidence and pride.
I often compare the things that you did
Back in the day,
And all that you did
Seems to have become my way.
All that I am is because of you,
And I'm sure you must agree.
Me and my mother,
Such strong black women, most definitely.

Chapter 3

"Comfort In Death"

YOU'RE IN GOOD HANDS

Dear mom,
I know you're in a better place but still you will be missed;
Your voice, your smile, your hugs
And your motherly kiss;
Now a memory, a memory that I hold
Dear to my heart.
You took care of me, stood by my side,
Loved me from the start.
And yes,
Your strength has made me strong.
Your honesty
Has taught me right from wrong.
Your caring
Has given me the ability to be kind.
Your knowledge of life
Has opened up my mind.
Now you're gone,
Standing by the Lord's side like you've always wanted to do.
I love you,
You're in good hands,
As I was with you.

<u>AUNTIE</u>

Auntie. . .
When I needed someone to listen
You gave me your ear
When I needed comfort
You wiped my tears
When I needed support
You lent me your hand
You gave without want
You gave without demand

Auntie. . .
When my faith wandered
You gave me guidance
When my spirit was weak
You gave me reassurance
When I questioned God
You took a stand
You gave without want
You gave without demand

Auntie. . .
I miss your laugh
I miss your smile
I miss your hugs
I miss your style
I miss your friendship
I miss your understanding
You gave without wanting
You gave without demanding
And I love you

LET ME GO

So much pain
So much sorrow
My mind was busy
What would happen tomorrow

But I looked to you Lord
Opened my heart
Spoke from my soul
Forgive me Father
Forgive my sins
Take away this pain
Please let it end
Now I stand by your side
Looking at your face
And I thank you
You are so merciful
So full of grace

Now I'm telling you
Don't cry
Smile
Wipe those tears from your eyes
There's no more pain
No more sorrow
I now have life everlasting
I no longer worry about tomorrow
I have walked through the gates of heaven
And oh. . .it's so beautiful
More than you could know
Don't grieve
Be happy
I'm doing just fine
Let me go

I'm in better place

ETERNAL LIFE

Don't think of me as gone
Because I'm not,
My eternal life has just begun.
I'm now home
In the presence of our Father
You know the almighty one.
The beauty that surrounds me
And the essence of his love is surreal.
Happiness and excitement
That I made it through the pearly gates
Is all that you should feel.
Comfort has now replaced pain,
Peaceful is my mind
When once I thought I was going insane,
And joy has replaced the sadness I was dealt.
So don't cry.
God has his arms around me
And I feel better than I've ever felt.

WONDERFULLY UNEXPLAINABLE

Look at me.
Look closely and you should see my smile.
There's no pain.
There's no tears.
I'm now walking heaven's golden mile,
And it's beautiful,
So peaceful,
A glorious delight.
Angels surround me.
I see friends and family to my left,
God on my right.
And when He said that He knew me
To explain the feeling I wouldn't know how to begin.
There isn't a word strong enough
To help you understand,
Help you comprehend.
Just know that I'm in a better place,
Happier than I could ever be.
Celebrate and be proud
Because I've made it to heaven
Where God's love now surrounds me.

GOD'S DANDELION

For years I admired the beauty of dandelions
as I walked through the park.
I never realized that such a tiny flower in my life
could represent a big part.
Starting out as a weed
I went through many trials and tribulations,
The other weeds in the world wouldn't allow me to blossom
by presenting so much temptation.
But the Lord reached out and held me
opening my petals giving me a golden glow.
As I loved Him I grew wiser; brighter. . .
the more I allowed myself to know.
As the Lord forgave me of my sins
my petals began to resemble a white cotton ball,
No matter which way the wind blew me
I shared my seeds of knowledge as they began to fall.
Now that my last seed has fallen
I blossom in heaven where peace and happiness flow.
So don't cry, I'm in a better place,
gather my seeds of wisdom and you too shall grow.

Sincerely,
God's Dandelion

I'M DOING JUST FINE

You're sad that I'm gone,
You think it's early but there was another plan.
There are some kids in heaven, who want someone to play with,
Hug or just to hold their hand.
My smile that you love
Is a smile that they need.
My laugh that you miss
Is a sound that they plead.
My hugs and affection that you crave
Are feelings that they desire.
All of those traits that you instilled in me
Is what the Lord desired.
Have faith in his plans
And I'll see you in due time.
I love you mommy and daddy.
I'm doing just fine.

REMEMBER

Remember the warmth of my hug,
The brightness of my smile,
My loving heart,
My exquisite style.
Please don't cry.
My time here was not put to waste.

Remember the way I laughed,
The way I played,
The songs we sang,
The nights we prayed.
Please don't cry.
Wipe those tears from your face.

Remember my words of encouragement,
My gentle touch,
How I've always been there for you,
How I loved you so much.
Please don't cry.
I'm in a better place.

Chapter 4

"Love-N-Such"

HELLO

Hello my love
I see you as I close my eyes
And you tiptoe into my dreams
Such a beautiful smile
Hello
Where have you been
I've been searching high and low
I know you were out there
At times I could feel your vibe
Our natural connection
Did you sit beside me on the bus
Did you walk pass me on the street
Did we share a place in line
Where were you
I know you were there
Hello
The wind delivers your voice to me
And I already know the comfort of the sound
The sun has gotten me accustomed to your warmth
The warmth of your arms
The warmth of your love
The warmth of just being near you
The sound of children
Laughing
Playing
Crying
Brings such joy to my heart
Because I know those wonderful sounds
Will play a significant part in our family
Hello
You're out there
I know you are
Walking with a stature that speaks confidence
Looking through eyes that see potential in all things
With hands that are strong enough to handle difficult tasks
But gentle enough to caress
And a mouth that speaks truth

Hello
I know you're there
And I'm here
Waiting
Hello

AS ONE

Two flames
Two hearts
Two minds
Two souls

Two flames
Two families
Now one as a whole

Sharing faith
and common goals
With binding love

Displayed before you
Our witnesses
And the Lord up above

United we are now
Like this single flame

United in life
United in name

Such joy right now
And it shall continue forever

Two flames
Now joined as one
Representing our future endeavors

Love as one
Share as one
Commit as one
Represent as one
And love God
The only one

NO LOVE UNTIL YOU RECEIVE HIM

Before you have me
You have to first receive Him
Our love will be put on hold
Until then
If you can't love God
You can't love me
If you can't talk to Him
How can you listen to me
Allow Him to lead your steps
So we can walk side by side
You have to take His hand
So He could be our guide
Lean on Him with your troubles
So our worries can be few
Learn to thank Him for everything
So He'll bless all we do
Make a commitment with God
So our love can begin
Before you can have me
You have to first receive Him

ETERNAL VOW

I walk down the aisle,
Everyone's eyes are on me.
At the end stands my love,
Looking as fine as can be.
Beside me is my father,
Which I'll soon part.
As he gives me away to the man
Who will take his place in fulfilling my heart.

The preacher reads the word of God
Once we're side by side,
Letting us both know
That the Lord will be there as our guide.
I look at his parents
Then look at mine.
Our love is a symbol of theirs
Brought together as one. . .forever entwined.

Finally we make our promises of
Trust, honesty and everlasting love,
Before our families, friends
And the Lord up above.
At last the preacher says,
"You may kiss the bride."
He places a kiss on my lips so tenderly
That my smile is hard to hide.

If it's possible for me to be happier
I couldn't tell you how.
Nothing's more pleasing than this,
Sharing an eternal vow

IT WOULD ONLY BE YOU

If I ever needed. . .
Someone to love me and hold me,
Someone to open up my eyes and help me see,
How much happier love could be.
It would only be you.

If I ever wanted. . .
Someone to kiss, squeeze and love,
Someone to always think and pray of,
As I talk to the wonderful Lord up above.
It would only be you.

If I ever had one wish. . .
For someone to share my heart,
For someone with whom I'd never part,
As if our love was a famous piece of art.
It would only be you.

If I ever could. . .
Marry someone who always makes me smile,
Who'd give me a good impression with a lot of style,
Who'd be by my side as I walked down the aisle.
It would only be you.

TOO SHY TO EXPLAIN MY FEELINGS

I love him very deeply
With all my heart and soul
And at times it's very hard
To explain my feelings for him
I know what I feel and want to say
But when it comes to speaking them
I choke on my words
Out of a sign of shyness

Deep down I want to tell him
That I care for him
That my life is basically
Based on him
That without him my happiness
Will no longer be there
And if he were to ever leave
I'd rather be dead

I want to tell him
That I need his motivation
I need him in my life forever
Even after death
And in heaven's happy world

The most important thing
That I want him to understand
Is that I love him
With all my heart

<u>HERE I AM</u>

A no nonsense woman
I have fixed me
Learned me
Adjusted me
To the Word
HERE I AM
I now have bible knowledge
Not worldly knowledge
I am heaven bound
Not earthly bound
HERE I AM
Standing in the light
No longer hiding in darken shame
Gave away my sins
So tired of playing the games
HERE I AM
Got tired of being found by the wrong ones
Chasing the wrong ones
Attracting the wrong ones
I'm ready to be found by my one
HERE I AM
Waiting for you

FIRST LOVE

That day when I first met you,
I couldn't believe it was really true.
There you were approaching me,
And I was thinking, "no it can't be."
Because a guy like yourself is considered a fantasy,
Something too good to be a part of me.
But it was true and you were there,
Whispering sweet nothings in my ear.
Then you reached down and slowly took my hand.
So clear you wanted to be my man.
At last we're together and joined by our hearts,
Keeping that promise of never being apart.
So now I give thanks to that man up above,
For helping me meet my very first love.

YOU MAKE ME FEEL

When I'm with you I feel as though
Nothing can go wrong.
When you hold me tight
I know our love is strong.
When you kiss me
You make me feel too weak to stand.
You drive me crazy
Just by the touch of your hand.

When I'm with you I feel as though
We were meant to be together.
Until death do us part
And in heaven forever.
When we talk to each other
Face to face,
I feel as though
No one could take your place.

You give me new feelings
With all the days,
You make me feel
All kinds of ways.

GIVE ME ONE MORE CHANCE

I'm really and truly sorry
That I hurt you again.
Please give me one more chance,
I don't want our love to end.
With a relationship
There is some bad,
But with each other
We shouldn't stay mad.
I feel our love and I'm trying my best
To stay true,
But the last time I did that
I had my heart broken in two.

Lately love
Has gotten me so confused,
With my past relationships
I've been nothing but used.
But you're different
And you're slowing changing my heart.
This is a relationship
I'm so scared to start.

I just need some time
To see if you're the right guy.
If I get hurt one more time
I swear I'll cry.
So please bear with me
Until I get used to your ways,
And I promise you
We'll have better days.

THAT'S LOVE

Sharing things
Being together
Making a commitment
That'll last forever
And that is love

Being a father
Being a mother
Having fun
With one another
And that is love

A relationship
Years gone by
Side by side
Even if one dies
And that is love

I MISS YOU

That day you left me I felt so alone.
You told me that you'd be back. You just had to go home.
It's been about a month but feels like a year,
Since I've seen you, don't you know I want you here?

Now I'm sitting here worrying about how you feel,
Because my heart is bleeding for you, I'm not lying this is for real.
I'm yearning for a hug and a simple little kiss,
But your love is the one I most definitely miss.

They say distance makes the heart grow strong,
But did they mean it had to last this long?
We have a great distance between us and I trust your love is true.
Please forgive me for worrying it's just that I miss and love you.

WHY DOES HE CRY?

Why do I see
Tears filling your eyes?
Did I hurt you,
Did I make you cry?
Whatever I did
Will you please forgive me?
Because if you don't
You'll make me feel guilty.

To see you in such pain
Really breaks my heart.
Tell me what's bothering you
Curiosity is tearing me apart.
If I did something wrong
Tell me so I'll do it right.
Oh please tell me,
This is going to bother me all night.

Is my love confusing you?
Is my heart bruising you?
Is there hate in my eyes?
Oh Lord help me out. . .
Why does he cry?

I HATE YOU

I hate you
Because to you this was nothing but a game.
You said your love for me would always remain the same.

I hate you
Because you left me in tears,
You said that our relationship would last for years.

I hate you
Because you broke my heart,
You told me that we'd never part.

I hate you
Because you lied to me,
You said for me you'll always be.

I hate you
Because you've given me pain,
You said you'd never leave me in the rain.

I hate you
Because you make me feel so sad,
You said with me you'd never be mad.

I hate you
Because you make me feel this way,
I hate you is a word I thought I'd never say.

PLEASE COME BACK

Last night as I laid in my bed
Right in front of me I saw your face.
It felt so real
That my heart went a quicker pace.
I saw a tear roll down your cheek
As you said you missed me.
And I woke up and thought
How lonely you must be.

Come back to me
Will you please come back to me?
Without you
You don't know how miserable I can be.
I feel so bad
Knowing you're so alone.
It's not enough
Talking to you on the phone.
I need to hold you
And listen to your voice.
You'd be with me now
If I had the choice.

Every night I dream
A little dream about you,
And every day I think about you
With all that I do.
Sometimes I lay across my bed
And cry,
As I think of all the pain
I went through to say bye.
Other times I sit and smile
With your picture in my hand,
As I think, out of all the girls in the world
You're my man.

So will you please, oh please
Come back to me?
Because I love you
And I need to feel your love for me.

POWERFUL LOVE

Everywhere I walk
It follows me

Every time I eat
It watches me

Every time I get hurt
It helps me

Every night that I sleep
It sleeps with me

Every day that I work
It strengthens me

Every time I get sick
It heals me

Every day that I'm sad
It comforts me

Isn't it wonderful
How powerful your love can be?

I THANK AND BLESS GOD

I smile as I think what our relationship
Is all about.
Going with you is like a maze,
Easy to get in but hard to get out.

Believe it or not
I like it this way,
Because it's with you and only you
That I want to stay.

I hope and pray
That we'll always stay together.
I wish love and happiness
Will remain with us forever.

As time passes by
As well as the years,
I'll always thank and bless God
For you my dear.

THE BETTER THE PAIR

The more we progress,
The more our love grows.
The more we think of each other,
The more it keeps us on our toes.
The more we give,
The more we share,
The more we stay true,
The better the pair.

I DO

Before God has united us as one in His own special way,
I'd like you to understand a few things if I may.
For one I sincerely love you with all my heart,
And the devil himself couldn't keep us apart.
For God has put us together and is guiding us by his light.
It's up to us to keep praying in order for everything to stay right.

Second of all, I'll never ever disrespect you.
As long as we're together, my love will remain true.
I'll never raise my hand to you in anger.
I'll never do anything to put you in danger.
I want you to always remember that I love you and only you.
Don't ever let our friends and family break us in two.
If we have disagreements let's talk them out with one another,
Not with the help of our father and mother.
If we have any problems we should keep them inside our walls.
Once insiders get in, that's when our love is bound to fall.

Finally, the phrase, "I do" when getting married means a great deal,
And since you've just said it, I know your love is real.
So now that I've gotten my point through,
Let's get on with this marriage. . .
"I do!"

I LOVE YOU

I love you!
I love you so much.
I love your smile, your hugs
As well as your touch.
I love the way you treat me. . .
So nice and sweet.
You're the kind of guy
Any girl would like to meet.

I love you!
I love you with all my heart.
I love you
Because I know you'll never break it apart.
I love the way you fill it
With happiness and joy.
I'll always be your girl,
You'll always be my boy.

I love you!
Yes, I love you so.
I love you because
I know you won't let me go.
I love our relationship
It has a lot of qualities.
I'll always adore you
Because I love the way you treat me.

MY SMILE

My smile means many things that I'd like you to know,
Some things are visible and others just don't show.
If I smile while you hug me
It means you're someone that I adore.
If I smile while you kiss me
It means I want more and more.
If I smile when you take my hand
It means I'm feeling fine.
If I smile when you say, "I love you"
It means I'm glad you're mine.
If I smile every second you're near me
It means I'm falling in love.
If I smile while we're in church
It means I'm thanking the Lord up above.
If I smile while I'm listening to a song
It means I'm thinking of you.
If I smile while I'm dreaming
It means I'm wishing it would come true.
If I'm smiling right now
It means you're a special man.
If you're smiling when you're finished
It means you understand.

I THANK GOD FOR YOU

I often wonder how I've come to meet someone as special as you.
You're sweet, kind, honest and independent in all that you do.
We met on a path that we in so many similar ways sought deep in our souls,
For someone to talk to, share love and at the same time hold.
If you haven't already noticed, I too indulge the feelings that you feel.
They're too hard to hide because they're not fake they're real.

When you stare at me your gaze is like a scorching fire,
Burning in search of my every thought and desire.
Your touch, like silk, runs so smooth over my skin,
Sending chills up my spine again and again.
Your kiss, so sweet, drives my soul wild,
Just the thought of these feelings makes me smile.

When I'm alone I fantasize of how it would be,
When I'm loving you and you're loving me.
These thoughts are so fulfilling when I'm down and out.
Me as your woman, now that's what I'm talking about!

Every night when I'm on my knees saying my prayers,
I thank God for always letting you be there,
With feelings of love and emotions so new.
To narrow this down sweetheart,
I love you.

NO ONE ELSE COULD COMPETE

Your touch so tender
And your kiss so sweet
Is something that I adore
No one else could compete
With your exquisite style
And feelings of love
You're someone special
Definitely sent from up above

Every time I hear the sweet sound
Of your voice
A smile comes on my face
Not intentionally but by choice
I enjoy every minute
That we spend together
As long as we live
Our friendship shall endeavor

Right now you have the key
To open the deepest depths of my heart
Cherish it forever
Don't abuse it
Please don't tear it apart
I trust you enough to know
You won't break my heart in two
To break this down evenly. . .
I love you.

THINGS WILL WORK OUT

Nothing comes easy
In this world today
We need a lot of prayer
For things to come our way

The devils waiting
Just to see us do wrong
We have to live a Christian life
To remain strong

We have a few months
To set up our life
For that big day to come
When we're husband and wife

Our wishes and needs
Don't worry about
The Lord is on our side
Things will work out.

THANK YOU FOR ALL YOU'VE DONE

I love your smile, I love your hugs,
I love your kiss and your touch.
I just wanted to say this
Because I don't say it as much.
For the past few days
I've been lying in my bed thinking,
"Does he notice this? Is he happy?
What is he thinking?"

I realize that sometimes
My love wanders away,
And I often realize
That I don't watch what I say.
There are days when I play around
And don't know when to stop,
There are days
When my smile just seems to drop.

Even though I sometimes get on your nerves
You still stand by me.
Those days when I want to play and you don't
You do it anyway to make me happy.

So I'd like to thank you
For the things that you do,
And I'd like to strongly say,
"I love you."

SWEET AND SPECIAL FRIEND

I often wonder what it would be like if we were together.
Would our relationship last forever and ever?
Could I make you happy with the love that I endeavor?
Could our love withstand any type of weather?
Even though we don't have a relationship
I repeat to myself again and again,
"To me you are a sweet and special friend."

At times when you get close to me I get this warm sensation inside,
And a smile so big that it's not even worth trying to hide.
When you stare at me and tightly hold me in your embrace,
Once again it's hard for me to wipe the smile from my face.
At nights when I lay in my bed
I repeat to myself again and again,
"To me you are a sweet and special friend."

I hope you understand that our friendship is something I'll always value,
As long as you are there for me I'll always be there for you.
The strong feelings I have for you could never stop.
You could never be rated because you're already on top.
And no matter what happens in our future
I'll always repeat to myself again and again,
"To me you are a sweet and special friend."

EXTRAORDINARY LOVE

There are times when you experience things in your life that are questionable.
How these things happened, you don't have an answer or clue.
If I can't remember any other experiences in my life,
I'm sure to remember one,
And that was the day when I unexpectedly met you.
Till this day I still can't figure out how we came to fall in love.
Our first kiss,
First date,
First words of love
Will be a special part of my memory.
I'll always cherish you in my heart as my first and only love.
It's like a dream or a wish come true that was always meant to be.
I want you to know that I would do anything to share my life with you forever.
I would gladly take you over all the money in the world.
All I ask of you is to stay with me always and fill my life with joy,
And in return I'll give you the chance to have me as your best friend,
Your wife,
And your one and only girl.

THE ROSE

You gave me a rose filled with love
Straight from your heart,
And I've kept it and cherished it
As if it were a famous piece of art.

To me it is priceless because
It came from you,
The first man in my life
That has made me feel so perfect. . .
So new.

So keep this petal and always remember
Its value to me.
This petal will fill a page of our life
And future to be.

AS HE SLEEPS

He's all the man that I want,
All the man that I adore.
He's perfect in so many spectacular ways,
Definitely what I was looking for.
His love is something that I'll always keep.
I think of these things as he sleeps.

He walked into my life
And kindly gave me his love.
He gave me something wonderful.
Something I'd only dream of.
His love is something that I'll always keep.
I think of these things as he sleeps.

He understands my wants
And understands my needs.
He shares my happiness
And answers my pleads.
His love is something that I'll always keep.
I think of these things as he sleeps.

He now holds the key to my heart
And I'm so glad we're together.
He's an answer from my prayers
And I'll cherish him forever.
His love is something that I'll always keep.
I think of these things as he sleeps.

GOODBYE

As we go off to work
In our own separate ways.
There goes another goodbye.

As we go off to visit family
And loved ones for a few days.
There goes another goodbye.

As we leave to go to the bank
Or simply to the store.
There goes another goodbye.

As we separate from one another
Every time we walk out that door.
There goes another goodbye.

As long as I know every time I leave
You're always there,
I have no problems with goodbyes.

But if these goodbyes get to the point
When they mean forever,
All else stops and I'm sure to die.

COLD SWEAT

As I walk down the street I feel lonely,
I feel there's something missing.
At nights I wake up in cold sweats
As I dream of the last time we were kissing.

When I go out to have fun like I used to
I always end up being bored.
At nights I wake up in cold sweats
As I dream of the times we went out and how they were adored.

As I'm working I think of you constantly, never my job.
My mind never stays in one place.
At nights I wake up in cold sweats
As I dream of how I used to finish my work to come home to your lovely face.

As I see other couples walking hand in hand
I picture it as being us exactly as they are.
At nights I wake up in cold sweats
As I dream of how we used to walk hand in hand under the stars.

Waking up at nights in a cold sweat away from you
Is starting to be a habit that I can't take control of.
But as long as it concerns you
It's a habit that I know I can learn to love.

OUR COMMITMENT

Together
You and me
Until death
Do us
Part.

Forever
Sharing love
From the
Deepest depths
Of our heart.

Always
Happy
As long
As we're
Side by side.

Eternal
Vows we keep
Until
We die.

WHERE, WHEN, HOW

Where would I be right now if I hadn't met you?
In a world lost in despair constantly feeling blue,
Amongst a crowd feeling lonely not knowing what to do,
Or condemned in a maze wondering what door to go through?

When would I have found love quite like yours?
As I grew old watching my life go out the door,
Two or three months after I was settled, maybe even four,
Or perhaps I would have never had this experience to adore?

How would I have known love without you showing me?
By going to a college majoring in a degree,
By seeing a therapist who would charge me a fee,
Or by reading books based on another's fantasy?

Where, when, how?
The answers to these questions are not important to me,
Because if I could answer any of them
Our love would never be.

MY MAN

So strong. . .
Is his mind
His heart
His love
The things in life that I'm most fond of

So tender. . .
Is his kiss
His hugs
His touch
The things in life that I miss so much

So true. . .
Is his thoughts
His dreams
His word
The things in life I mostly deserve

So right. . .
For me to have
To keep
To understand
The one thing in my life
My man

I PROMISE

I promise
To forever keep you happy
For the rest of your life.

I promise
To be your friend
Your lover
As well as your wife.

I promise
To be there when you need me
Through pain and sorrow.

I promise
To love you today
And even more tomorrow.

I promise
To be with you
In every accomplishment that you make.

I promise
To be by your side
With every step that you take.

I promise
To keep our love on the up-n-up
And never on the down.

I promise
To forever be faithful
And never fool around.

I promise
To remain as your better half
And never act as a leader.

I promise
Myself to you and all that I'm worth
Because in us I'm a believer.

GOTTA BE A SIN

I look at him
And quickly look away
The thoughts that run through my mind
Oh let me pray.
The temptation is strong
No, I can't let it win
The way he makes me feel is unnatural
It's gotta be a sin!

To kiss him would be a dream
Merely set my soul on fire
To make love to him would be a fantasy
A pleasant thought and desire.
The temptation is strong
No, I can't let it win
The way he makes me feel is unnatural
It's gotta be a sin!

I took the chance
But I tried and tried
What's done is done
It can't be denied.
The temptation was strong
I had to let it win
The feelings were unbearable
It was definitely a sin!

ALL YOU WANT

Tell me you want me
And I'll give you a star.
Say you'll forever be true
And I'll surprise you by far.

Tell me you love me
And I'll give you the world.
Share with me your hearts desires
And I'm forever your girl.

Stay forever mine
And I'll give you the moon.
Say you'll marry me
And I'll sing you a tune.

Share with me your innermost secrets
And I'll give you the clouds up above.
Always be there for me
And I'll give you my love.

KEEP PEDALING

I'm riding my new bike
Which took me awhile to learn.
To get it on a steady pace
Was my biggest concern.
I'll ride it on the roughest road
Or up the steepest hill.
I'll ride it when it's old
Or when it's on its last wheel.
You see, our love is like a bike,
Riding and passing despair and hate.
We have to keep pedaling
Because to stop would be our fate.

DEATH WITHOUT MY LOVE

I enter his room
He's soundly asleep
To me he's so beautiful
His heart I'll forever keep
I kneel beside his bed
To look in his face
He looks as if he's been crying
What could cause this disgrace
In his hand he holds my picture
Around his neck is my ring
He's lying on my clothes
I wonder what's happening
I know we're happy together
I know our love is strong
We have nothing but good times
What's going on
I reach out to wake him
But my hand disappears
I jump back in shock
It's exactly how it appears
No it can't be
I slowly look up above
So this is how it is
Death without my love

CAN YOU

Can you feel it?
Can you feel the pain my heart is going
Through right now?
Being away from you is unbearable.
I don't know how to maintain.
Can you tell me how?

The tears keep falling,
Constantly running down.
Can you wipe them from my face?
Can you hear my prayers,
As I pray that the love I share and give
Is not a waste?

If there's any other way
For me to prove and show my love,
Can you tell me what to do?
Can you relate to my feelings;
Take me to higher levels;
Be with me forever?
Tell me. . .
Can you?

I NEED YOU

There's no one here to hold me
When I'm feeling sad.
There's no one here to share my joy
When I'm feeling glad.
There's no one here to make me laugh
When I'm feeling down.
There's no one here with whom
I can play and fool around.

There's no one here to shower me with kisses
From time to time.
There's no one here to embrace me
As we lay entwined.
There's no one here to make me feel
So good or so new.
There's no one here to love me
Quite the way you do.

Baby. . .
I need you!

TO WANT MY LOVE

To want my love. . .
You have to be in need
And willing to give.
You have to be truthful
And able to forgive.
You need to be honest
And full of caring.
You need to be trustworthy
And content with sharing.
You should be strong in will
And passionate in heart.
You should be gratified with desire
And honed to start.
You could have all of me
If you can fulfill the above.
You can have my heart
If you want my love.

FALLING TEARS

I close my eyes
Dream that you're here
There's no stopping
The falling tears

I pray to the Lord
That he keeps you near
There's no stopping
The falling tears

Deep in my heart
I hold you dear
There's no stopping
The falling tears

I miss you gravely
Hope you soon appear
There's no stopping
The falling tears

Forever yours
Today, tomorrow on through the years
There's no stopping
The falling tears

BEAUTIFUL EYES

I look up to see my reflection before me,
Surrounded by love, kindness and unnatural beauty.
It's being held by personal will and not by force.
I feel special to be there.
I show no remorse.
Every glance that I take puts me in a daze.
Visions of joy come to me in so many ways.
Visions of everlasting trust and caring.
Visions of a bond that could be daring.
Visions of things I'm unable to speak.
Let me stop, I'm feeling a little weak.
It's amazing how the words seem to fly,
When I look deep into your beautiful eyes.

HOLD ME

Am I dreaming?
Or am I actually here?
I've been away for a few months
But it felt like a year.
I missed you baby. . .
More than words can explain.
It was torture without you.
It was hard to maintain.
You kept my love strong
By showing you care,
By words of love,
By just being there.
Now we're together again
And I'm happier than you could know.
Just hold me
And never let me go.

TENDER KISS

Flames burn deep within,
Chills run up and down my skin,
Feelings so good I'm unable to dismiss.
I'm addicted to your tender kiss.

A sensation I've always yearned to seek,
Capable of making me oh so weak,
I never knew I could feel like this.
I'm addicted to your tender kiss.

Upon my lips the memory still lies,
Deep in my heart and right before my eyes,
A memory that I cherish and miss.
I'm addicted to your tender kiss.

ALL SEASONS

Our winter love can be one of warmth and delight.
Sitting by the fire, holding each other tight.
Sharing Christmas joy,
Play in the snow.
Making angels,
Sneaking a kiss under the mistletoe.

Our spring love can be one of new growth and beginning.
Like the flowers that bloom, the beauty is never ending.
Growing together as one, learning new things.
Dancing to the joys of life as nature sings.

Our summer love can be one of happiness and fun.
Full of passion like the rising sun.
Sitting on the beach, walking through the park.
Adventure during the day and party when it's dark.

Our fall love can be as colorful as the falling leaves.
As ongoing and deep as the distant seas.
Like a beaver building a safe and cuddly den,
We'll build a stronger love to live out the seasons once again.

AS I'M UNDERWAY

Thinking of you
Every night and day.
My love for you is stronger
Than words can say.
Memories of you
Come more than one way,
How we used to laugh, talk
And sometimes play.
Wish you were beside me
As I lay.
Ask for your well-being
When I pray.
In my heart
Is where you'll always stay.
These thoughts come daily,
As I'm underway.

THINKING OF YOU

You're in my heart
In my mind
I'm thinking of you
All the time

You're in my prayers
In my dreams
I'm thinking of you
On the highest extreme

You're in my goals
In my plans
I'm thinking of you
And it's all so grand

You're in my beginning
In my end
I'm thinking of you
A constant trend

ALL THE THINGS THAT I MISS

Your words of love
The way you care
Your sexy smile
The things we share
Waking up in your arms
Walking through the nights
Your beautiful eyes in the morning
The way you hold me tight
Your passionate love
Your sweet and tender kiss
The glow of your smile

All the things that I miss

WILL YOU BE MY VALENTINE

You've come into my life
And brightened up my days.
You've made me smile
In so many different ways.
The love that we share
Is so sweet and kind.
Will you always be
My sweet valentine?

We started out as friends
And have grown as one.
The happiness that we share
Has just begun.
The love that we have
Is so genuine.
Will you always be
My sweet valentine?

I gave you my heart
To cherish and hold.
I gave you my love
Which is more precious than diamonds and gold.
What we have
Is so hard to define.
Will you always be
My sweet valentine?

I only want you
And nothing more.
To share with me a life
That I've always wished for.
So I'm asking you
Just one more time.
Will you always be
My sweet valentine?

TO BE LOVED

To be loved
Is to be with you!

To be held
Makes me feel wanted forever.

To be kissed
Makes me feel we're one together.

To be touched
Makes me feel cherished and adored.

To be loved
Makes me feel like I have something to live for.

To be praised
Makes me feel responsible and smart.

To be happy
Makes me feel that I've made the right choice from the start.

To be proud
Makes me feel that my man is the best.

To be loved
Makes me feel that I don't have to worry about the rest.

To be satisfied
Makes me feel that no other can please.

To be married
Makes me feel as your wife, so much at ease.

To be energetic
Makes me feel that you are my strength when you're near.

To be safe
Makes me feel that I'll never have a fear.

To be loved
Is to be with you!

TO HAVE A CHILD

To have a child is. . .
To have someone you can love and hold;
To have a life in your hands to shape and mold;
To have someone look at you with admiration and joy;
To have someone to watch grow into a big girl or boy.

To have a child is. . .
To have a second part of you;
To have someone to care for as they learn from the things you do;
To have someone who appreciates your every move;
To have the feeling of responsibility that you don't have to prove.

To have a child. . .
Growing inside of you will show you how beautiful life can be;
It will bring forth a life that will make you say,
"This lovely child has come from me;"
You will learn all their wants; you will learn all their needs;
To have a child one day for all these reasons is what I pray for indeed.

LONELY

Lonely in my heart
Lonely in my mind
Lonely when I'm near you
Lonely all the time
And it hurts
Yes, it hurts so bad
To not feel your love
Leaves me feeling sad
I know I'm selfish
When it comes to your love
I want it all now
Even when I'm in heaven above
I hate feeling lonely
When you're right by my side
It feels like my heart has stopped beating
And something in me died
At night I pray
That we keep what we started
I pray we stay together
Cause anything else will leave me brokenhearted

ALWAYS NEAR

At times you feel down
Because I'm not by your side.
You feel the distance that separates us
Is just too wide.

There are days when you feel
Depressions going to do you in.
You feel the tears that fall
Will never come to an end.

Sadness comes more often
Than ever before.
A need for my companionship
Grows more and more.

I know these feelings are unbearable
But please don't you fear.
I may be away from you physically
But my love is always near.

SO FAR AWAY

Missing. . .
Thinking. . .
Needing. . .
And you are so far away.

Desiring. . .
Loving. . .
Wanting. . .
But you are so far away.

Lonely. . .
Worrying. . .
Hating. . .
That you are so far away.

STICKING TOGETHER

So often we argue about such petty things.
Many times we express joy in songs that we sing.
Every day we show our love with a hug or touch.
Occasionally we say things that hurt so much.

So often we share things that bring us joy.
Many times we have conversations of having a girl or boy.
Every night before we sleep we end it with,
"Goodnight, I love you."
Occasionally we don't show the other attention which makes us feel blue.

Many people are unable to go through these things and stick it out.
That's why our love is so strong
Because sticking together is what we're all about.

HERE I GO AGAIN

Here I go again
My biggest fear
Arguing and fighting
Bringing back the tears
A painful relationship
I prayed nothing would go wrong
But her I am
Singing another sad song

Here I go again
My heart is in pain
Here I go again
Hiding my tears in the rain

Here I go again
My strongest thought
The lies he told
The lies I brought
Another woman
Holding my man
Used to be my man
Can you understand

Here I go again
Taking his word
Here I go again
Single and as free as a bird

Here I go again
Searching for love
Wishing and fantasizing
Praying for help up above
Thinking I should leave it
Walk by
Go home
Life is too short
Don't want to be alone

Here I go again
Not knowing what to do
Here I go again
Looking for love in you

HOW SWEET IT IS

You are my motivation
A soulful inspiration
My sun when it rains
My strength when in pain
Yes baby, you are my all in all forever
Me and you will always remain together.

Just two
Me and you, how sweet it is
Not three
You and me, how sweet it is

I'll be your provider
Help you open your heart a little wider
I'll bring you joy
Be your man. . .no need to be coy
Yes baby, I'll be your world
Standing by your side
My number one girl

Just two
Me and you, how sweet it is
Not three
You and me, how sweet it is

One on one
Having fun
Side by side
I'll be your guide
Hand in hand
Only we can understand
How sweet it is
Yeah baby
How sweet it is

Just two
Me and you, how sweet it is
Not three
You and me, how sweet it is

YOU HURT ME

You hurt me
The abusive words
And constant fights
The continuous insults
Waking to be alone at night
You hurt me

No more respect
And all the lies
Bringing hate in my heart
Tears to my eyes
You hurt me

Stopped the kisses
Stopped the caresses
No more making love
That left me breathless
You hurt me

The other woman
I saw by your side
The hotel receipts
The numbers you tried to hide
You hurt me

Begging for my forgiveness
Claiming to be my only man
Wanting me to take you back
Hoping I'd understand
You hurt me
Never again.

DESERVE BETTER

Numbers, gifts, pictures and letters.
Boy, I thought you knew me better.
What does she have to make you disrespect me?
Tell me something, help me see.
Cause I'm hurtin' right now.
I don't know what to believe.
I've been in this situation before,
I had to leave.
This will hurt worse because I gave you
My heart, mind and soul.
I even changed my personality to please you,
That was my goal.
Yes, my attitude has changed
Cause that trust that was taken took a piece of my heart too.
All that you see now is a result of what you put me through.

My mind's wandering,
The wall's back up,
Can't come in.
That hurt and pain
No. . .no. . .no. . .
It can't happen again.
A miracle would have to happen to bring back that trust.
For us to stay together,
That miracle is a must.
I love you,
But not enough to destroy my life.
I deserve better
As your friend and wife.

US

Laughing,
Curious,
Playful,
Well mannered,
Romantic.
When we first met.

Loving,
Happy,
Proud,
Planning for the future.
When we were married.

Unhappy,
Lonely,
Scared,
Tears,
Looking at the past.
When we celebrated our anniversary.

DON'T WASTE MY TIME

What are your feelings?
Where's your mind?
You brought mine out just to tell me yours will take time.
Look, I'm not ready for the run around; can't take the games.
I'm looking for someone to meet me on my level,
Someone to feel the same.
My heart is valuable, you know; can't be given to anyone.
I'm holding it on lock down until I meet that special one.
Is it you?
Can you tell me; do you know what you want?
Be straight forward, I'm a grown woman, don't front.
I'd rather know than waste my time on a love that's not there.
I've been hurt too many times for you to see any tears.
So run it on me sweetie.
There'll be no hard feelings; no hard words.
You look like a straight forward person, at least that's what I heard.
So is this hi,
Or should I say so long, goodbye?
Give me some answers, I'm here,
Standing by.

SPECIAL TOUCH

It's been year's baby. Can you believe it?
Time fly's when you're having fun.
It's only been a few years;
filled with ups and downs, tears and laughter
and our life has just begun.
You've made my life wonderful and made me happier
Than anyone could ever be.
You're a great father, wonderful husband and a very good friend.
All of this I hope you see.

I love having your lips upon mine, being held in your embrace
Or holding hands under the moonlight.
I enjoy our talks, look forward to your laughter
And love the way you keep me in your sight.
You complete me more than you could ever imagine,
More than you could ever know.
I'm so glad we found each other, so glad we're still together
And I pray we'll never let one another go.

You've given me kids, my life new meaning and happiness;
For this I thank you so much.
I hope from these words on our anniversary day you understand
That our happiness is the outcome of your special touch.

OUR ANNIVERSARY

Our first date. . .
Do you remember?
The first time we kissed, made love. . .
Do you remember?
Our children definitely sent from up above. . .
I say again, do you remember?

All of these special times run through my mind as we celebrate this day,
And to think we have many more coming our way.
God has a tight grip on our marriage,
Nothing can tear it apart.
You see, we're a living example that love can make it
If you keep Him in your heart.

With the tears we're still able to smile.
Yes, we're holding on.
With the arguments we're still able to laugh.
Yes, we remain strong.
With the ups and downs we're still able to pray.
Yes, we still have that spiritual bond.

So many years and counting,
How blessed can that be?
Just know that I'm thanking you right now
For the life, love and happiness that you've given me
as we celebrate our anniversary.

THE MEANING OF LOVE & MARRIAGE IS YOU

Love is. . .
Being up when there are downs,
Smiling when there are frowns,
Having words when they need to be heard
Or having answers when problems occur.

Marriage is. . .
Love combined with a bond that's never ending,
Being by that person's side from the beginning,
Providing support, inspiration and affection with every breath,
Having only one partner from the days vows were spoken until
You are parted by death.

Once everyone understands this,
Many marriages will reflect yours.
You're a living testimony that this and a strong faith in God
Will give your life more.
We're all here today to share your joy but at the same time learn.
So please except our happiness and praises
It was most definitely earned.

Happy Anniversary

THE MEANING OF US

Your smile is my joy,
Your tears bring me pain,
Your hands provide protection,
Your happiness is my gain.

My heart you have,
My love you hold,
Your eyes are my guide,
Your warmth takes away the cold.

Our paths are led by the Lord,
Your steps have been my guide,
Your love held us together,
Your accomplishments have been my pride.

The years have been wonderful,
The future holds many more,
Today on our anniversary,
I hope you realize how we are adored.

LONELY WOMAN

Silence
Not a word spoken
Two people in a room
I'm by myself
Lonely
Two hearts side by side
Only mine beats
Sadness overcomes me
Hurt stabs me
Tears dare to fall over
This is where our love has come
I'm with you

BEAUTIFUL THING

You fall in love,
Then you're set apart.
You reunite,
Then you're set apart,
But the distance between you
Just strengthens your heart.
Yes love is a beautiful thing.

You marry young,
People frown.
You marry young,
They put you down,
But the bond is real
And you're still around.
Yes love is a beautiful thing.

You argue and fight
But you love her so.
You disagree and cry
But you love him so.
In difficult times
True love won't allow you to let go.
Yes love is a beautiful thing.

Such lovely kids,
Yes you have been blessed.
Together for so many years,
Yes you have been blessed.
Your love is still growing,
You've passed many tests.
Yes love is a beautiful thing
And we see this in you.

LOVE

Bonded
Sealed
Two becomes one
Love

The perfect feeling
Perfect kiss
Completeness
Love

Thoughts known
Secrets no more
One mind
Love

New love
Perfect love
Eternal love
Yours

LOVE SHOULD BE

Love should be. . .
Pure, binding, natural. . .
You guys definitely have that flavor.
Your smile is brighter,
The vibe is empowering,
It all shows in your behavior.

Hold him,
Love him,
Embrace her,
Adore her,
Let your love flow.

Communicate,
Encourage,
Spend time together;
Those special moments
Let your love grow.

Like now,
We see,
Not two but one
Growing strongly.

Allow this moment to move through you
Like the rhythm of a song.
We're proud of you, glad to be a part of this day,
May your marriage remain strong.

HOLD ON AND EMBRACE

"Cry"
And those tears are wiped away.

"Angry"
And you end up smiling in that same day.

"Empty"
But filled when you're together.

"Discouraged"
But encouraged when you think what you have in each other.

Hold on to that man, embrace that woman!

"Laugh"
At the lines that were used when you first met.

"Smile"
As you remember all the dates that were set.

"Vision"
The first time you made love and how you felt.

"Hear"
Those words of endearment that made your body melt.

Hold on to that man, embrace that woman!

"Enjoy"
Today, tomorrow and the future years.

"Appreciate"
The good times. . .the memories; hold them near.

"Continue"
To communicate and work things out.

"Always"
Love through the ups and downs because that's what marriage is all about.

Hold on to that man and embrace that woman!

WHAT IS IT

You used to hold me
But now you rarely touch me
What is it

Not a day went by without you kissing my lips
Now that feeling has become a memory
What is it

To make love to me is something you constantly craved
Now it seems that taste is lost
What is it

Conversations came easy
Now words are no more
What is it

Your smile was contagious
But it seems I'm the only one left smiling
What is it

With our relationship there were never any worries
Now I constantly question us
What is it
Can you tell me please

STILL THE SAME

You don't trust me with all that I do?
I trust you, so why is that so hard for you?
Since you put this ring on my finger
You've been acting strange.
Is there something that I did
To cause this change?
I'm still the same woman
That you met from the beginning.
You know the one that said
Her love for you will be never ending.
I want you to know
That there is only room for you by my side
I'm not doing anything to hurt you,
I have nothing to hide.
Let's talk and fix whatever's on your mind,
Whatever's in your heart.
Should this problem conquer our love
And break us apart?

WANT MY FAMILY

Don't you know I love you?
I would do anything for you and the kids.
Right now I'm hurting,
Wondering what's going through your head.
What could I have done
To cause this change?
Where is that woman that I married?
Who are you?
You're not the same.
You've left our home, said some untrue things,
Took my girls.
You know I love them more than anything,
Would do anything. . .
they are my world.
Lord knows I don't know what this is
But we can get through this together.
I hold to my promise
For better or worse, till death do us part,
True love forever.
This situation has brought me to my lowest,
Made me view things in a different way.
Never will I take for granted
Love. . .
Life. . .
I just want my family back
For this I pray.

WE HAVE THE LOVE

Love. . .
That's what we have
Love at first sight

There are no expressions
There are no words
There is no wrong and there is no right

We'll make mistakes
And we will learn

We'll have arguments
And forgiveness we'll yearn

We'll cry
But we'll also laugh

We'll hate
But share joy on each other's behalf

Baby. . .
The size or value of a gift could never
Describe your love for me

What you do and share from your heart
Is of more importance to me

Each moment that we share
Whether it's good or bad
I hold dear

Baby we were meant to be
It's our destiny
And I have no fear

This ring shows that I am thankful
To have you in my life
I proudly wear it on my hand

This ring also holds a special stone
Which symbolizes the heart
Of a very special man

And I'll love you always

YOU MY MAN

You
my man
have been
wonderful to me

You've made me laugh
like no other
my smile bright
as can be

And I thank you
thank you for the joy
thank you for the caring

Thank you for loving me
holding me
and sharing

These years
have been wonderful
I look forward to our future
because I've enjoyed the past

This love that we share
is strong
unbreakable
definitely made to last

And I love you

UNITED AS ONE

Individually
We laughed
We dreamed
We cried
We set goals

Individually. . .
Like these candles
Two minds, two hearts,
Two souls

Separate lives
Leaning towards family for comfort
Confiding in friends for support

But now we have each other
We have established our own special rapport

Now one
Like the flame on this candle
Together joined
One team

Laughter will be shared
Comfort will be given
Goals are now combined
And bigger are our dreams

Our love
Our relationship
We hand over to God to shape, mold and provide direction

Before you
As our witnesses
We promise an eternal connection

GETTING MARRIED

We've been friends for many, many years.
Shared laughter, shared joy
As well as tears.
And now this moment. . .
You're getting married.
Wow!
I can't think of a moment I've seen you happier
Than you are now.
And I'm proud of you.
No one is more deserving of the love that you are receiving.
I pray that it will continually grow
And you'll allow God to do all the leading.
And as you go on to your new journey
And this new chapter in your life begins,
Always remember that I'm here for you,
I will always have your back
As your sistergirl, sisterfriend.

LOVE'S SEARCH

Aimlessly I searched for my missing piece
Was it him
Nah
Did he fit
Nah
But he's kind of close
Let me give him a try
No match
I cried
But I searched again
For my soul mate
My friend
Would my loneliness end
Single forever was so hard to comprehend
But then I prayed
And stopped crying
Prayed
And stopped looking
Prayed
And you found me
Never knew my searching caused you to lose me
You turned left
I turned right
You took one step
I took two
Always out of reach
Always out of sight
But you prayed
Lord let her be still
Lead me to her
If it's your will
And you found me
Now our love is sealed
Your rib is over my heart
Perfect match
Perfect fit
Completeness
Single no more
We found what we were looking for

I'M SORRY

Baby, I'm sorry.
I know there's no excuse that can be given to you,
Nor will I insult you
By making something up like most men do.
I was foolish.
Downright dumb.
What I did was beneficial to none.
But now I see my thoughtless actions
Have hurt you. . .hurt us.
Now I'm asking for your forgiveness,
I desire to win back your trust.

The hurt in your eyes
Gave me more pain than I could bear.
Any other punishment that could be given
Could not compare,
To the lowness and the shame
That's tearing me apart.
Please forgive me, don't let go,
You're my everything,
you're my heart,
And I'm sorry.

STEPS OF LOVE

When you first met there was something
A look
A touch
A word
A song that you heard
Then there was LOVE
Then you decided
To make it forever
Becoming
One heart
One mind
One soul
United together as a whole
Making LOVE
Creating a child
Children
A blessing
Bundle of joy
Extension of oneself
Yourselves
Building life in LOVE
Through age and many changes
Schedules
The kids
Tears
Unpredictable years
This will challenge LOVE
But a strong foundation in GOD
Laughter
Communication
Prayer
Affection
Your unique connection
Will keep LOVE

I GIVE THIS RING

I give this ring to you because
I want to see
Every sunrise. . .sunset
The glow of the moon
The twinkle of the stars
Places that I've never been before
Only with you

I give this ring to you because
I want to hear
The lovely sound of your voice
Your continuous words of endearment
Your laughter
The first cries of our child
Only with you

I give this ring to you because
I want to feel
The love that you give me as a man
The warmth of your touch
The passion in your kiss
The strength of our togetherness
Only with you

I give this ring to you because
I want to have
A piece of heaven here on earth
A lifetime of memories
My puzzle complete
My forever
Only with you

MY HEAVEN ON EARTH

I look in your eyes and see
How much you care for me
Adore me. . .love me
I see your dreams
And understand what they mean
Cause they mirror mine
And that's just fine
We're walking this path together
Same journey as one forever.
Yes, I looked in your eyes and saw
"My heaven on earth"

I hear your voice,
Words spoken, promises never broken
Ideas always open
You heard us, spoke us
Brought two parts together as one. . .us
I hear your heart song
Making right all the wrong
Thoughts I had about love
You're truly sent from up above
Yes, I heard you
"My sound of heaven on earth"

I acknowledge and know
That your love is true
That I can trust you in all that you do
God has sent you to me
And we were truly meant to be
One. . .
In soul, body and mind
We will stand the test of time
I can sincerely say that I cherish
You, us, our children. . .this marriage
Yes, I honestly know
"You're my piece of heaven on earth"
And I thank God for you

LET IT BE

I reach, I pull, I struggle
With no reciprocation
I kiss, I love, I hug
With no participation
And it hurts
Where has the love gone
And I cry
Where have we gone wrong
There's no more holding
An invisible line between our bed
There's no more affection
The chemistry between us is dead
And I'm confused
Without God I would feel so alone
I call on Him
Help my marriage, heal my heart, rebuild my home
I'm at the end of my road
The fight has left me
I give it to you Lord
Whatever your will. . .let it be

I DON'T KNOW WHY

I see that you're cheating
But I don't know why
I hear your dishonest words
But I don't know why
I feel that your love isn't true
And still I don't know why

Why did you marry me
Profess your love to me
Then go out and commit adultery
Why

Why do you not come home at night
The constant fights
As you blame me for not doing right
Why

Why the constant lies
A different story as the days go by
You can't look me in my eyes
Why

Why is there a missing connection
Lack of affection
I feel we're living in deception
Why

I see
I hear
I feel
And I know
But I don't know why

LOVE, WHAT HAPPENED

You're supposed to love me
Not act like you don't care
Ignore that I'm here
Not speak
That's so unfair
What happened to compassion
The attraction
Desire, in some form or fashion
What changed between you and me
What are you seeing that I don't see
What can it be
I'm clueless and lost
I'm hurting and for what cost
Love lost
Why
Give me a reason
It feels like we're changing with the season
When it used to be pleasing
I want it back now
Just tell me how
I love us. . .I love you
As I stated in our vows

WHAT DO YOU DO

I'm standing on the edge
Close to falling over
I reach for you
Grab for you
Hoping to be able to hold on
But as I reach you push
You turn away
With no words
Passion gone
Feelings no longer strong
Like my strength to continue
To force your love
So I lift up my hands
And let go
Do you catch me
Or let me fall

I KNEW

From the moment you touched my hand,
I knew you'd be the one to understand.

From the moment you looked in my eyes,
I knew you'd be the one where my passion lies.

The moment I heard the sound of your voice,
I knew you'd be the one; the right choice.

The moment we couldn't stand to be apart,
I knew you'd be the one whose rib was over my heart.

MISSING YOU

I heard our song today and it brought tears to my eyes,
and I realized that even when you want it to, time never fly's.
I miss you baby.
Your kiss. . .your touch,
hearing you say that you love me so much.
Even the smell of your cologne,
I just want you home,
in my presence; in my sight forever.
This distance is such a hard endeavor.
But I will continue to pray
for your safe return back to me.
I just want you to know that I'm missing you baby
and waiting patiently.

AM I WORTHY

I walked in and saw your smile
The sound of your voice put me in a trance
And I wondered
Could I ever get the chance
To get to know you
Learn your likes; learn your hates
Take you out to eat or a movie
You know, a date
Yes, you caught my attention
I'm not going to lie
I had to let you know
I couldn't let you go by
I'm stepping out on faith
To see what might come our way
Am I worthy of a chance
What do you say

Chapter 5

"Think About It"

WHAT SEASON ARE YOU IN

Are you in a summer season
Heated and full of hate
Sweating with envy
Dehydrated with fate
Parched for lust for someone other than your mate
You've lost your thirst for Him
Feel it's too late

Are you in a fall season
Where you'll fall for anything
And can't seem to stand upright
You've hit rock bottom
And have lost all sight
Of what is wrong and what is right
You just want to stay down and quit
For Him you've lost the fight

Are you in a winter season
Where your emotions are frozen solid
And your heart is cold
Your youth is melting away
You feel so old
The warmth of your soul is now frigid
And for faith you no longer have a hold
You heard of His everlasting love
But you no longer believe what you were told

Or have you jumped into spring
Where a new heart is blooming
And your belief has grown
You've given Him your problems
And you no longer weep and moan
He now steers your life and it's beautiful
You no longer set the tone
A new spirit within you has blossomed
And you now claim His love as your own

Think about it. . .
What season are you in

YOUR OWN FIX

You fall
Then you rush to pick yourself back up
You hurt again
So you patch your wounds with a bigger bandage
You're broke
So you create a hustle
You cry
But allow the enemy to remove your tears
You're lonely
So you seek the wrong friends
You want light
But you're searching in darkness
You desire to speak properly
But you allow your tongue to control you
You're loveless
So you form a fake heart to become attractive
You reach for Jesus
But at the same time you're grasping sin
You try to fix it all on your own
But I can't help you
Until you let go and let me

YOUR ACTIONS

Child, help me understand why you didn't accept that person's apology
Then help me understand how your actions exhibit me
Did I not forgive your lies
Wipe those tears from your eyes
Grab your hand and lift you up
Give you strength when you were about to give up
I remembered your name when you forgot mine
When the doctor said you were going to die, who gave you more time
Yes me, Jesus, the one who forgave you for all that you did
The one who said it's alright, now lift up your head
Go out and share your testimony, tell them what I've done
I was looking forward to hearing how many souls you've won
But instead you became selfish, a little cocky even
You forgot that you're not perfect, you were only portraying an image that's deceiving
Your love should have mirrored mine for all, not only those you choose
Well child, I no longer forgive you
Your actions have caused you to lose

YOU'RE ALL MESSED UP

You suffer from pain
Because you speak it.
You're broke
Because you don't tithe, you keep it.
You're lost
Because your spirit has no direction.
You're damaged
Because you won't accept protection.
You cry
Because you won't allow your heart to grow.
You stay in trouble
Because of friends you won't let go.
You can't keep a job
Because you disrespect your leaders.
You lack knowledge
Because you refuse to be a reader.
In short, you're all messed up
Because you're unwilling to learn.
Instead of accepting Jesus and being obedient,
You'd rather burn.

A MESSAGE FROM YOUR FRIEND

I saw a friend of yours today
He said He hasn't spoken to you in years
He said you used to talk often
You'd lean on Him in comfort
Read together
Dance and even sing
But as time went by
You started to pull away
You became too busy
And found new friends
He says that He still sees you from time to time
But the happy person He once knew
Has disappeared
But don't worry
He forgives you and still wants to be your friend
He's just concerned that you may have forgotten His name
But He remembers yours
So He told me to whisper in your ear
And tell you to give Him a call
He's available anytime. . .day or night
His name is
Jesus

LET ME LEAD YOU

Why should I beg you to come to church?
Why should I beg you to do what's right?
I only continue because God's telling me,
"Don't give up without a fight."
I see your pain.
I see your hurt.
It's like all that you go through is written on your shirt,
Visible for all to see,
As they shake their heads in pity,
But still you won't listen to me
When I tell you about my Jesus;
How He'll fix it all.
He'll lift you up. . .heal you
Never allow you to fall.
All you have to do is come before Him,
Give Him your heart,
Accept Him in faith and He'll give you a new start,
In this life that He has given us
There's no reason to fear,
To suffer with unnecessary pain and cry those unwanted tears.
Stop trying to fix it yourself and listen to me,
Take my hand and let me lead you to our Jesus
Whose love is more than you'll ever see.

WHO AM I LOOKING AT

Mommy,
Why is it when we go to church
You're shouting "Amens"
Throwing up your hands
Thanking God for what He did
But Friday night
You could hardly get out of bed
From going out hanging with your friends
You could barely walk
Your words hard to comprehend
We see you differently
At home you always look mean
But in church you smile
On the road you're cussing
But in church you're waving as you walk down the aisles
Monday through Saturday we listen to secular music
As you drop it like it's hot
Only in church do we hear Christian music
And then you barely rock
The Pastor has always told us
That a true Christian will never straddle the fence
You got one hand slapping the devil a high five
And the other reaching for repentance
So I'm saying this as your child to let you know
That your behavior has me confused
Am I looking up to a mother who loves the Lord
Or a woman who's world abused

I SIT, THINK & CONTEMPLATE

I sit
Think
And I contemplate
How we in life can help motivate
Change
From the old to the new
Get rid of the things we're accustomed to
Appreciate this land
That God created for man
From the dirt beneath our feet
To the rising of the sun
To that person next to you
Realizing that we're one
In God's eyes
Sisters and brothers
How we can go through life
Hurting one another
It's so hard to comprehend
We need to change our characters
Remove the sin
Alter our steps
Walk in a new day
Increase our knowledge
So we can speak in a new way
That will provide wisdom
That will give life to the generation coming
We're bound by so much technology
It's mind numbing
Words no longer spoken
Time rarely spent
No one knows
Where interaction went
Hands
No longer reach
Eyes
No longer seek
Goals
No longer met
In God

We forget
We must change
Rearrange
The path that we're taking
Analyze
The decisions that we're making
Respect the woman
Honor the man
Be kind to your neighbor
Love your children
Remember the more you give in love
The more you'll receive
Once we establish these principles
There's nothing we can't achieve
Change
Life. . .
Heart. . .
Soul. . .
Make this our goal
To not
Would be a mistake
I sit
Think
And I contemplate

TELL ME HOW YOU REALLY FEEL

They talk about my personality. . .
But they don't know me.
They talk about my looks. . .
But who are they?
I'm your friend,
Your wife,
Your soul mate.
What do you see?
Do I cramp your style?
Do I give off negative vibes?
Do I bore you?
WHAT!
Tell me your perception of me.
That's all that matters. . .somewhat.
What they think holds no importance to me.
I know my heart is big,
I know my mind is strong,
I know I have a caring soul,
And God loves me.
What bothers me
Is your voicing others opinions
Instead of putting them in their place
Cutting them off
And correcting their thoughts.
What's really going on?
How do you really feel?
We both said "I do"
After we both said "I see"
This in her or him;
After we both said "I love"
This in her or him;
After we both said "I feel"
This in her or him;
So what's up?
I'm hurt,
I'm confused,
And I'm frustrated.
You need to talk.
Tell me how you really feel.

THERE'S NO GREATER LOVE

Our Father,
Gave up His only Son
To die for something he didn't do!
All because He cared for us,
Loved us.
Could you?
Could he?
Could she?
No one would,
No one will.
There is no greater love than our Father's!

Daily
He sees all of our sins,
Hears the evil thoughts,
Witness' destruction.
And still He forgives us,
Forgives all.
Could you tolerate
The visions;
The sounds;
The disaster?
No one would,
No one will.
There is no greater love than our Father's!

All He wants from us
Is to believe and have faith.
Talk to Him,
Acknowledge Him,
Love Him!
Don't be too busy.
Show some respect
And reciprocate what He's given.
All of us should,
Honestly say you will,
Because there is no greater love than our Father's!

FORGIVE

Your husband had a baby
By another lady
Now you're crying tears
Thinking all the wasted years
Who is this man you thought you knew
Having a secret lover he lied to you
Now he had the nerve to apologize
So ashamed he can't look you in your eyes
Says he didn't mean it
It was a big mistake
You look to God
How much more do I have to take
But I know it's hard the pain you had to hide
You held it all in
You cried and cried
But you have to forgive
You have to forgive so that you can live
You don't want to hold on to all he did
You have to forgive
God wants you to live
Forgive

Your child was murdered
You have to identify the body
You're full of rage
Wondering how can anybody
Kill your child
Do such a sin
You hate that person
All you want is revenge
As you go to bed
Evil thoughts run through your head
Your family fell apart
Cause you've had a change of heart
You spend all your time thinking what you're gonna do
To this evil person that really hurt you
You hate them
You want their life to end
But I know it's hard the pain you had to hide

You held it all in
You cried and cried
But you have to forgive
You have to forgive so that you can live
He'll take care of what they did
You have to forgive
God wants you to live
Forgive

Your father was abusive
He treated you bad
He said you were the child
He wished he never had
You went out of your way
To try to please him
No matter what you did
He wouldn't give in
He wanted you out of his sight
You constantly had to fight
This went on for so long
You're thinking what's the problem
What is going on
You didn't know what to call it
Your mother said he was an alcoholic
The damage is done
You hate him so much
You don't care for his love
Or even his touch
But I know it's hard
The pain you had to hide
You held it all in
You cried and cried
But you have to forgive
You have to forgive so that you can live
He had a sickness
He doesn't know what he did
You have to forgive
God wants you to live
Forgive
So that you can live
You have to forgive

LOSE THE TRADITIONS

I can't go to church
They stay there for hours on end.
I can't go to that church
Because they are too straightforward and talk about sin.
I can't go to that church
They make me stand too long.
I can't go to that church
They speak in tongues and speak of prospering
All of that is wrong.
I can't go to that church
Because there is no structure and they don't follow a program.
I can't go to that church
Because they praise out loud and they even have a band.

Wow!
Traditions will hurt you,
Now I say stop all your whining and complaining.
You're leading yourself down the path of hell
By the traditions you're sustaining.
You teach without scripture
And praise your own name,
Causing people to leave
Because of your petty gossip in which you see no shame,
Worrying about time
Instead of allowing time for my spirit to touch all,
Using my name to make money
Causing your soul as well as others to fall.
Instead of being humble with your possessions
You allow them to possess you,
All I want is for you to praise me
Speak my name
What else do I have to do?
It's written in word,
Was shown in signs
And still you don't follow through.
Lose the traditions,
Get rid of the formalities,
Love me as I love you.

HOW IS IT

Tell me,
How is it one can see and feel God's glory
Then turn back to sin?

Why would you want to go back
To where you began?

There is no hiding,
There are no secrets
Your life to Him is always open.

Our God is fully aware
He's always listenin'.

I hope you realize
He's coming back again.

Only He knows the time;
Only He knows when.

Don't turn your back on God
Because when the wrath comes
It could be your end.

Hold on to God's love,
A soul with no faith
Is twice as hard to mend.

WHAT MOTIVATES YOU

What motivates you?
Is it satisfying your kid's wants instead of their needs?
Is it those depressing newspaper articles you constantly read?
Is it that model on TV whose image you're trying to duplicate?
Or is it pleasing a man whose goal is to see how many hearts he can break?

What motivates you?
Is it your desire to achieve at work no matter the consequences?
Is it your hope to become rich under all the wrong circumstances?
Is it your dream to obtain an abundance of possessions which has no worth in God's eyes?
Or is it your fantasy to see the world for enjoyment when you could be using that opportunity to spread His name for miles?

Think about it, where do you fall in?
If you want a prosperous life,
having God as your motivator is where to begin.
He will take care of your children's needs
and your desire to read the paper and watch the news will end.
He will allow your soul to shine to the point everyone will desire to look like you,
And your soul mate wouldn't have to be searched out,
God would create a path that would lead him straight to you.
He'll give you so much favor at work that promotions will become abundant
and bonuses will flow.
Your desire to become wealthy will no longer be a priority
because you'll be rich at heart and possess a wealthy soul.

Worldly motivations are short lived
and serve no purpose whatsoever,
Godly motivations are long lasting,
give you purpose
And joy forever.

HOW CAN YOU

How is it that you want God to put you first
When you put him last all the time?
How can you ask God to give you something
When you can't share a dime?
How can you ask Him to take away your pain
When you don't comfort others?
How can you ask God for children
When you don't respect your father and mother?
How can you ask Him to give you knowledge
When you don't study the bible?
How can you say God "I worship you"
When you give more praise to false idols?
How can you ask God for money
When you don't give your 10% or tithes?
How can you ask God to believe you
When you're so full of lies?
How can you ask God to touch your heart
When you have it surrounded by walls?
How can God talk to you
When you never give Him a call?
How can you ask God to give you a job
When you won't do His works for Him?
How can you ask God to forget your past
When you tightly hold on to your sins?

Tell me, how can you?
Instead of saying, "can you, can you, can you."
You need to start saying,
"I will, I will, I will."

HE CAN FIX IT

I awoke to the noise and the words.
The insults, the cursing, and then her crying;
Yes, that's what I heard.
Then you hit her
And she fell to her knees.
You stood over her
And she said, "no more please!"
Did you have mercy?
No! You had to deliver one more hit.
The look on her face told me she had enough
This was it.
While you were sleep,
I watched her get the gun.
There was nothing that I could do when she pulled the trigger
I was so young.
I was so angry then.
I didn't understand.
How could mom kill you?
My dad. . .her man.
I was alone and scared
When they took her to jail.
I was part of the system now and I hated her;
My life pure hell.
As I grew older, became wiser
I was able to forgive.
I had a relationship that mirrored the life
My mother once lived.
But unlike her I didn't use violence
I called on God who took my hand.
He gave me the strength to get help, take my children
And leave that man.
For this I thank Him.
He was my strength and my healer,
Got me through it all.
He too can be your help,
All you have to do is reach out and give Him a call.
Think about your life, think about your children.
Is it really worth it?
God is powerful.

God is awesome.
Whatever your ordeal
He can fix it.

WE NEED GOD

Families are falling apart
Leaving the household disturbed
Kids are acting out
communication is scarce
No one speaks a word
One parent plays two
The kids feel alone
No one prays anymore
We need God back in our homes

Schools are no longer safe
More frequent there are fights
Disease among our children is running rampant
Their futures don't look too bright
Students are disrespectful
No one follows the rules
The structure is fallen apart
We need God back in our schools

At work it's all about money
Customer service is dying
Employees are shooting up their jobs
We have a problem, there is no denying
Now we wonder why people are
Frustrated, stressed or just two-faced
There's only one truth
We need to bring God back into the workplace

God says
You need to take me back into your life
Put me in your everyday living
So that you may once again have peace
I am forgiving

YOU WILL BE PUNISHED

You were supposed to teach them
Not turn them away
Your life was to be an example
Now you've led them astray
You were to collect tithes
In honor of my name
Instead you gave my name a price for your benefit
I bow my head in shame
I forgave all
But hurtfully you set limitations
Your mind should have been on me
But you were blinded by temptations
Your punishment will be tenfold
When you stand before me
Your sinful joy will be short
You lived your life wastefully

BLOCKING YOUR BLESSING

Please listen closely,
And don't take this the wrong way.
But as a friend who cares about you
I have a few things I'd like to say.
Will you please let go of that man?
You deserve so much more.
You are taking a path of heartache.
What do you want that for?
While you are holding on to him
You could be blocking your blessing.
Mr. Right might have been right there
But now he's gone, isn't that depressing?
So what you don't want to get married!
So what you don't want to have kids!
You still have a heart
And your feelings aren't dead.
You are a beautiful woman
With a strong mind.
So why settle for someone already taken
Being the other woman all the time?
There are too many men out here
With ulterior motives playing games.
We as women need to have more respect
And be unwilling to accept anything that can cause us shame.
You ask me
Should you take a chance with another?
Yes! Get rid of him girl.
He's a no good brother.
Try that one who's available
And has a sincere interest in you.
Loose that extra baggage and I truly believe
That God has something in store for you.

I DON'T CARE

I don't care about your past
I'm looking at the now
If I'm not questioning it
You shouldn't be asking the why, what or how
I don't care how you dress
Your shirt, pants or shoes
Just claim me
Let me be the one you choose
I don't care how much money you have
What you accomplished doesn't appease me
I care that you praise me,
Love me, honor me
Do you hear me
Acknowledge me
You've sinned
Well all of you have
All of you will
You think you're not worthy
You all have worth in my heart
You all will receive your fill
Just ask for forgiveness
Become a witness
I love you all the same
Remember
I don't care what you used to do
From this day forth
Live by my word and claim my name

DRUGS BE REMOVED

Please make it stop.
They're calling my name.
I can't handle this alone.
I'm going insane.
The devil is busy.
He's making me weak.
I need you now Lord,
Right now, this minute as we speak.
I've caused my mom to cry,
My dad to disown me.
My friends no longer want
Anything to do with me.
I'm asking you for strength
For my mind, body and soul.
Please remove these drugs from my life
And make me whole.

TRY AND TRIED

I try, try and try,
And wonder why,
I even have to. . .why?
It's like I'm living a lie.
Do I smile or cry?
Hang on or say bye?
What changed to make the affection die?
Why can't you look me in my eyes?
Acknowledge me when I say hi?
Am I your enemy or bride?
It's not only about you, but you and I.
I tried, tried and tried.

A WOMAN

I am a strong and beautiful woman
And I will not allow you to degrade me.
When you think about it
Without us where would you be?
Who do you think gave you life?
A woman!
If and when you get married who will you call your wife?
A woman!
Who is that person you call mom and love?
A woman!
Who gave birth to the son of the Lord up above?
A woman!
Who's able to take care of their children with just an hours rest?
A woman!
When everyone sees the worse in you who still sees your best?
A woman!
When you want to cry without insult who do you run to?
A woman!
Who can manage the home, family, job and even you?
A woman!
Other than you who else can dribble, kick, catch or hit a ball?
A woman!
You're good at your job but who else do you think would give it their all?
A woman!
If you're capable of learning I know who else can?
A woman!
God created us to be one with the man.
Yes women!
We are strong and beautiful!
Do not degrade us again!

AREN'T YOU PROUD OF ME MOMMA

I saw him hit you everyday
I heard him curse at you as I laid
I saw your beautiful hair turn an instant gray
I now have a man who loves me the same way
Aren't you proud of me momma

I saw the black eyes as he called you a whore
I heard him tell you not to step a foot out that door
I watched you run to your phone when he called because to miss it would be war
I now have a man who protects me like yours
Aren't you proud of me momma

I saw him control your mind like you didn't have a clue
I heard him demean your character and tell you what to do
I watched you change into somebody that no one knew
I now have a man that runs my life too
Aren't you proud of me momma
I'm going to be just like you

DANDELION

Your beauty surrounds me
I'm so amazed
It's so empowering
I'm left in a daze
As I walk in your presence
So free is my mind
The world has stopped moving
I lose track of time
Your scent calms me
Your brightness lifts me
A little piece of heaven
This has to be
All of these feelings are real
Because I know I'm not dyin'
You are so, so beautiful. . .
dandelion

A PIECE OF ART

Before me
My reflection
A disaster
Rarely a perfection
I'm too big
Supposed to be thin
My hair is long
But short is in
Turn to the side
Too much butt
Ok. . .breathe in. . .hold it
Now I can't see my gut
Long skirt won't do
Short will put me in someone's view
Put on some makeup
Gloss these lips
Put on my favorite belt
That defines these hips
Still not satisfied
Hate what I see
God what happened
Why did you make me so ugly

Dear child look in that mirror
Through the eyes of mine
Don't you know that everything I touch
Is uniquely designed
Love yourself
As I love you
The world's image
Will distort your view
Use those eyes
To see your spirit within
Your weight will not be a deciding factor
When I come again
Lift your face to me
Whether it's done or not
Through those lips sing songs of praise
With all you've got

Left and right move those hips
Big or small
As you dance in worship
Do give it your all
Each of you were made different
Created from my heart
You're not ugly
You're unique
A piece of art.

TERRIBLE WORLD

This world is terrible and it gets worse with every year.
I know the Lord looks upon us and sheds a tear.

We have terrorists blowing themselves up and hijacking planes.
We tighten our security but they can't be stopped, they're mentally insane.
They take our buildings, blow up trains and schools.
When evil lurks and takes a grip there are no rules.

Women are sleeping with women and men with men,
Families are falling apart and fathers are sleeping with their children.
Children are being kidnapped, raped, murdered and abused.
And if you don't want children there's not only contraceptives,
but abortions are being used.

Families are mixed up. It's no longer mom, dad and kids.
Now it's baby momma, baby daddy, step mom, step dad and step kids.
Punishments for doing wrong no longer fits the crime.
When things go wrong the fault is someone else's, no longer mine.
Prayer is forsaken and speaking of the Lord will get you fired.
We look forward to hearing the latest news but to hear the word of God
There is no desire.

This world is terrible and it's getting worse with every year.
Just know the Lord looks upon us and he's shedding tears.

<u>DO YOU</u>

Don't worry about the others
Not your sister
Your brother
Your dad
Your mother
Do you

It's not what she thinks
It's what you think
It's not what he thinks
It's what you think
Do you

Your decision
Your choice
Your vision
Your voice
Do you
And be happy

WHY

I dream of someone holding me
But it's not you

I dream of someone kissing me
But it's not you

I dream of passionate words spoken softly in my ear
Those whispers did not come from you

I dream of taking walks, laughing and talking
But you weren't by my side

I dream of being touched and caressed
But those hands were not yours

I dream of someone showing me remarkable love and I yell out
But your name did not come out of my mouth

Why

THE OTHER MAN

I try to get my man's attention
But he pushes me away.
The other man begs to give me attention
With every passing day.

I try to give my man a tender and passionate kiss.
He turns his head.
The other man says he'd die for a kiss.
It's in his prayers before he goes to bed.

I try to get my man to hold me or keep me near.
He says I'm taking up his space.
The other man promises he'd never let me go,
If I'd just let him put me in his embrace.

I try to get my man to talk to me.
He cuts me off and puts me down.
The other man gives me much needed conversation
Whenever he sees me around.

My man, whom I love dearly, doesn't see
That I crave for his attention, his love and his touch.
Why is it the other man who I don't desire
Tries so hard to give me the things I need so much?

GET OUT WHILE YOU CAN

The first argument you broke my nose.
You left me there wondering, "Is this the man I chose?"
I called my best friend, she told me to leave.
I told her I couldn't, for this to happen again is hard to believe.

He came back into my life on bended knees.
Said he just lost it, had a lot on his mind, this was his plea.
I love this man. I had to give him another chance.
Now my loved ones won't even give me a second glance.

We're still together. Two months have gone by.
I'm in the hospital with a broken arm and two black eyes.
My best friend is beside me and says as she cries,
"Please leave this fool, you could have died."

Did I listen? Of course not, I love this man.
I told my family to leave us alone,
They don't understand.
He says no one else will love me,
No one else will be there for me,
Everything that has happened was my fault. Now I'm feeling guilty.

A few months have gone by and I come home late.
He's angry; I smell liquor on his breath. He asks was I on a date.
I tell him no. I tell him that I only love him.
He punches me in the face and says,
"Girl, you know you're lyin'!"

I feel weightless. I feel like I'm dreaming. I move toward the light.
I see my whole life flash before me and then I see a shocking sight.
Everyone that really loved me is dressed in black and I hear crying sounds.
Their heads are bowed as a casket is lowered into the ground.
The preacher than says, "Bless the daughter of. . ."
And I hear him say my parent's name.

I jump back in shock. This has to be a game.
I run to my mother but went right through her falling to the ground.
Oh God! If I had only listened I would have turned my life around.

If you're ever in a relationship that's abusive and degrading,
Get out while you can. Use me as an example of what could be waiting.

DON'T WANT TO HEAR IT

Your child talks back; he's being rude,
He doesn't listen; he skips school,
His grades are slippin'; his homework is never done,
Instead of payin' attention, he's all about havin' fun.
Stop!
I don't want to heart it!

She's wearin' too much makeup,
Look at the color of her hair,
Those pants are too low; you can see her underwear,
Her mouth is filthy; every other word is a curse,
Are those condoms in her purse?
Stop!
I don't want to hear it!

He's sellin' drugs, robbin' stores, look he doesn't care.
She has two kids and one on the way, just a teenager on welfare.
He hits his mother, has a record, been in jail for various crimes.
She smokes weed, has sex for money, she's been with more than one man at a time.
Stop!
I don't want to hear it!

No!
I don't want to hear it!
I'm tellin' you like you told me.
I can't spank them, I can't punish them,
I'll mess up their personality.
I'm lettin' them make decisions, letting them have a mind of their own.
So now that things have gone bad,
Stop blowin' up my phone!
This is the world that you've created; don't put it on me,
You're the one changin' the rules, tellin' me how to raise my family.
Parents stood up and tried to bring this to your attention,
"I don't want to hear it," is what you'd say.
Now I'm tellin' you,
"I don't want to hear it!"
All we can do now is pray.

DEPRESSED

I woke up this morning
And right away I knew it was one of those days.
You know,
When you're feeling bad in a whole bunch of different ways.
Your mind starts wandering
As you think about things you normally don't.
You try to stop and get back to reality
But you can't and won't.
Then you have those that ask you,
"What's wrong? Are you feeling alright?"
And others telling you that you look nice
When you know you look a sight.

It's funny when you can't ask yourself what is wrong.
You try to go out with friends and have fun
But you feel like you don't belong.
Sometimes you feel so bad
That you feel the need to cry.
But it seems like no tears come as you try and try.
Once again you're sitting there
Trying to figure out how this sadness came.
You feel kind of dumb and think you're going insane.

You'd feel a whole lot better
If you could get what's bothering you off your chest,
But that's impossible when you wake up
Feeling depressed.

WHY MY WEDDING DAY

And hour goes by.
He's still not here.
I know he's coming.
He'll soon appear.
People are getting
Impatient and mad.
I dare not turn
To look at my dad.

Another hour goes by.
People start to leave.
My hope is gone.
I drop to my knees.
The tears fall constantly,
One after another.
I look up and before me
Stands my mother.

"Why?
Why must my heart
Be broken this way?
Why must this happen
On my wedding day?"

ATTITUDE

A person's posture or pose,
The day their bad side shows.
Their good side seems to be dormant,
So their appearance seems to be ignorant.
Everyone has these days,
So I guess you can call it a phase.
This is my way to forewarn,
That everyday a person like this is born.

I'M JUST A CHILD

Oh no
I'm pregnant
I don't know which way to go
My parents will hate me
I don't want to let them know
They'll look down on me
Call me names
They already assume I think
Life's a game
Just one time
Having sex without protection
Will he leave me
Will this baby give us a love or hate connection
I refuse to get rid of it
He or she has no say
Why me
I'm just a child
I wish I could take back that day
Lord I pray
That you please help me get through this endeavor
I pray that this one mistake
Won't ruin my life forever
Help me to make the right decisions
From this point on
My sins please forgive them
I want them gone
Lord I want you to guide me
I'm giving you my hand
I know that only you can ease my heartache,
Take away my confusion and understand

WILL YOU BE BY MY SIDE

Listen to my word,
Feel my praise.
My return is coming,
No one knows the day.
Worship me,
Honor my name.
When judgment comes
I'll do the same.
Your sins are forgiven,
Your pain is no more.
Heartache and loneliness,
You'll no longer endure.

I have died for you,
Shed blood for you,
Even when you doubted
If any of this was true.
Just pray and believe
Is all I ask.
Read my word and follow my commandments.
Is this such a hard task?
For you to have another chance
Is why I died.
When the day comes
Will you be by my side?

I USED TO WONDER

I used to wonder why
Women would stay
Only to leave
After the children have gone away
But now I can see
How some can hang on
For the children
With hopes that they don't see any wrong
Vacant love
Passionless nights
Words unspoken
Wondering how things
Can be right
These thoughts hurt
When you have no clue
Of what changed
What you're supposed to do
You've heard the same from friends
But at that moment
Couldn't comprehend
How two people in love
Could fall apart
When the same two used to be
One at heart
But now you're living it
And can see
The same things I used to wonder about
Are happening to me

SELFISH

How can people be so SELFISH; be so mean?
I get so frustrated with their actions that I just want to scream.

A woman abandons her children just to get high,
Now the state has taken them and they're wondering why,
Mommy has left them to be surrounded by strangers.
They grow up feeling not wanted, so full of anger.
Were the drugs really worth losing your children;
Worth the change in their life?
Was it really worth the pain, heartache and strife?
"SELFISH"

A pastor sleeps with another man's wife
Letting temptation win.
He preaches the word, a wolf in disguise,
Heart full of sin.
Many are confused by his actions and most leave the church.
The lost go back to sin and the strong do a faith search.
Was that night of passion worth losing souls?
You were supposed to lead by example,
Help make them whole.
"SELFISH"

A girl looks for love in all the wrong places.
She goes from men to men putting on many faces.
She wants to be grown when she's really just a child.
Her reputation is ruined and her body's defiled.
Now she's pregnant, about to have a baby;
Was being an adult really that fun?
Was it worth the abortion you're now getting
Because you feel you can no longer run?
"SELFISH"

A boy joins a gang because he wants to feel cool.
He thinks he's smarter than those telling him to stop,
So he drops out of school.
He starts selling drugs and a few lives he take,
Now he's behind bars for life and he can't say it was a mistake.
His story has made the front page.

Do you think he's feeling cool? Do you think he's feeling fame?
Were the crimes really worth everyone knowing his name?
"SELFISH"

Stop being so SELFISH; stop being so mean?
I'm so frustrated with your actions that I just want to scream.

CPSIA information can be obtained at www.ICGtesting.com
Printed in the USA
BVOW061642130912

300312BV00006B/1/P